TAMING THE TIGER PARENT

Tanith Carey

ROBINSON

ROBINSON

First published in Great Britain
by Robinson in 2014

Copyright © Tanith Carey, 2014

The moral right of the author has been asserted.

A CIP catalogue record for this book
is available from the British Library.

ISBN: 978-1-84528-549-4 (paperback)
ISBN: 978-1-84528-564-7 (ebook)

Typeset in Adobe Caslon Pro by PJM Design
Printed and bound in Great Britain by CPI Group

Robinson
is an imprint of
Constable & Robinson Ltd
100 Victoria Embankment
London EC4Y 0DY

An Hachette UK Company
www.hachette.co.uk

www.constablerobinson.com

CONTENTS

INTRODUCTION

JOHN WAS JUST FOUR days old when his mother Dana set about teaching him to read.

The fact that newborns can't focus on anything more than a few inches away – let alone recognise words – did not deter her. Dana was so evangelical in her belief that sooner is better that twice a day she ran through a set of ten flashcards with her firstborn son.

'I would show John words like "milk", give him my breast and then show him the baby sign language for milk,' says Dana, a 41-year-old American businesswoman who had relocated to the UK. 'I did it every morning and evening. At first I did it so he would get familiar with the sounds – and then so he could see the shape of the word.'

Dana – who moved on to teach John meditation and scientific plant classification – says: 'Of course, when he was first born, I knew he couldn't see the words, but he could hear them and I thought it wouldn't do any harm.'

By nine months, Dana says that John was pointing and using baby sign language to show he could recognise up to twenty words and phrases including 'I love you', 'nose', 'ear' and 'arms up'.

No matter that the programme Dana used, 'Your Baby Can Read', has been censured by consumer watchdogs for falsely inflating parents' expectations. Or, that after sales of £112 million around the world in four years, the firm has now gone out of business after experts pointed out that there are just as many dogs as babies on YouTube who, when given a simple word, can correctly point to the right flashcard.

Like every mother, Dana simply believes she is doing the very best for her child. 'It's survival of the fittest,' she explains without apology. 'I want to give my son every mechanism out there to get ahead of the pack. In eighteen years, John will be at either Yale or Oxford. You'll see.'

In fact in today's increasingly cut-throat race for Oxbridge or the Ivy League, some might even consider that by waiting until John's birth, Dana has left it a little late. We live in a culture where mothers go on pre-conception diets to boost brain power, and where über-organised couples time the moment of conception precisely in order to give birth just after the 1 September cut-off date for schools.

Savvy parents know that, due to being the oldest in the school year, autumn babies are off to such a flying start that they end up twenty-five per cent more likely to get a place at Oxford or Cambridge. So perhaps it's no coincidence that, over the last decade, September and October have been consistently among the three most popular months to give birth in England and Wales.

No sooner has sperm successfully met egg than mothers turn their wombs into their children's first classrooms. Unborn babies become the captive audience for classical music blasted in utero in stereo – before they even have ears. Once safely delivered, infants have barely drawn their first breath before parents are fretting about their Apgar scores. Under starter's orders, the curriculum proper now begins: flashcards before infants can properly see, baby sign language classes before they can talk and baby swimming classes before they can walk.

Yet, extreme as it all sounds, when I interviewed Dana and dozens like her, I have to admit I understood where she was coming from. After all, I too had given birth in a culture where, from the moment the umbilical cord is cut, parents like me live with the constant fear that they can never do enough to make their offspring the brightest and best.

As the mother of two children, I will start this exploration into the causes and effects of tiger parenting by confessing that, like so many others, I too had succumbed to the message that child-rearing was a race. When my first daughter was born almost thirteen years ago, her future seemed mapped out. I approached my new role with more dedication than I would an MA. This was to be my ultimate test. For the sake of my daughter, I could not fail. If there was an enrichment programme, toy or book I could use to make my baby smarter, I would try it. I would play so much Mozart that the synapses in her tiny infant brain would fizzle and pop. I would breastfeed until she reached her optimum IQ.

In dismay, I looked back on my own childhood of benign neglect, complaining that I had simply been left to 'go and play' as if that were tantamount to child abuse. Never mind that my happiest memories were of kicking the branches of the fir tree that hung above my garden swing and tapping the heads of frogs in the garden pond with sticks. All that was conveniently forgotten now that I had joined the educational arms race.

When my baby arrived in December 2001, all went to plan. I loved the way her eyes seemed to sparkle with amazement when I jiggled and turned her in her baby sling to look at works of art in museums and art galleries. At moments like those, I felt like the best mother in the world. After all, I was told there was not a moment to waste. The neural explosion in the brain, which started at conception, would abruptly stop at the age of three.

Soon my bookshelf groaned under the weight of books with titles like *Make Your Child Brilliant* and *Bring Out the Genius in Your Child*. On the first day at Montessori, I glowed with satisfaction when, while other toddlers dashed about, my daughter quietly sat down and arranged the right number of plastic pigs in the correct red circles. Naïvely, I assumed all my hard work had paid off.

But of course, this was just an early skirmish. The culture had not only had its effect on me but also on every other parent I came across.

Six months later, we returned from two years living in the US to the UK, where my husband and I had been working as foreign correspondents. By a stroke of luck – and I suspect my husband's charm offensive on the school secretary – we managed to find my daughter a place at an over-subscribed private nursery. There I found myself just one of many mums and dads all locked in the same frantic race to get ahead. As a first-time mother arriving from abroad, I knew nothing of the Machiavellian ways of modern parenting.

Innocently, I assumed the next step would be the girls' school round the corner when my daughter was four. My bubble burst when, over coffee halfway through the first term, another mother broke the news: 'Well, you know there are four girls trying for every place, don't you?'

Gripped by panic, I tried to catch up. Information was traded with other novice mums in the same boat. Neurosis underpinned every conversation at the school gates, particularly as all of us had the same goal. Bit by bit, I caught on to the dark arts of pushy parenting. I spied the tell-tale yellow plastic Kumon folders concealed inside rolled-up *Grazia*s in rivals' handbags – and signed my daughter up myself. The latest intelligence was passed along in hushed tones: 'Did you hear that Sarah (just turned four) can write half a side of A4?' 'Have you heard that Yasmin (three and a half) is reading chapter books on her own?' By stealth and persistence, I wheedled out the name of the top tutor in the area, only to find she had a two-year waiting list. Still I was a rank amateur compared with the other heat-seeking missiles I was up against.

One day, when my daughter came home from a playdate, I asked her in the car on the way back what games she and her friend had played. She reeled off the usual list of activities – hide-and-seek, princesses, trampolining – before adding: 'And Alexandra's mum gave me a spelling test.'

But children are not pet monkeys to be trained to perform in a circus. In order to win at competitive parenting, you have to have a child who is willing to come along for the ride. Behind closed doors, my home was fast moving away from the oasis of fun and security I had intended it to be. Instead of enjoying playing with my now five-year-old for her own sake, I found our free time together had become an endless round of worksheets and educational games. I couldn't even bake cupcakes without wanting to turn the exercise into a teachable moment to talk about weighing and measuring.

Although my husband Anthony and I had consciously tried to shield our daughter from any expectations, she had quickly cottoned on to the message that life was one endless competition. An innately modest child, she simply decided she did not want to be constantly measured and compared with other children for everything she did. The alarm bells started ringing in Year Two when, after I personally made sure she turned in the best space project, she won the end-of-year prize.

While I applauded uproariously from the sidelines, she fled the room in tears and refused to accept the £10 book token from the head teacher. When she calmed down, all she could say was that she hated us making a fuss. What is just as likely is that she resented the fact that her successes had become as much ours as hers. Even at that young age, she realised that the more she succeeded, the more pressure she was under to keep it up.

By the age of seven, it was becoming clear how much our daughter's self-worth had been affected by the hothoused environment which engulfed her. Because she felt she had to be good at everything, she didn't think there was any point trying at all. Worse, she saw me as part of the problem, always expecting me to expect more. To her childish eyes, instead of just seeing me as her mother, she had also come to see me as an extension of an overbearing school system. She stopped looking me in the eye and became more tense and irritable. Abruptly, I changed direction and took my foot off the gas. Gradually we repaired our relationship. With my second child, I had learnt my lesson – and she was less stressed as a result.

Aware, as a parenting journalist, that the same thing was happening in other families too, over the next three years I interviewed educators, parents, child psychologists and teenagers who had come through the competitive education system. What struck me most was the scale of the emotional fallout for parents and children alike.

One of the people I met was Jenny Foster, a former teacher and neurolinguistic programming practictioner, who had set up an organisation called Inner Sense to help some of the children who were casualties. Jenny is one of a growing body of professionals who believes pressure on children to perform at an early age means they develop so much anxiety that learning stops getting through to them – in other words the exact opposite of what tiger parenting sets out to achieve. The youngest child she has seen is six.

She explained that children are not helped by the increasingly narrow focus on targets and league tables in schools at the expense of play; play, which even in the most brutal times for children in history, has intuitively been recognised as an essential part of growing up. But with so much pressure bearing down on schools from above – from both government and global rankings – there is also less time for subjects in which children who do not excel in the most tested subjects of Maths and English can prove their worth.

The more target-driven schools become to keep up with the

international competition, the less opportunity there is for children to develop skills like emotional intelligence and empathy. The less time there is too for them to learn about themselves and how to interact with others, leading to a rise in behaviour problems and mental health issues.

It's not just the sensitive children who don't relish a contest who are the cast-offs. It's also the youngsters who, at first, appear to cope well in this winner-takes-all system; the ones who come to develop perfectionist tendencies, and who grow to believe that their worth is based on test scores and have to spend their time defending their positions as top dogs in the classroom.

☆ ☆ ☆

It is both the best of times and the worst of times for our children. The tragedy of all this over-investment is that we are *not* producing a brave new world of brighter, more accomplished, wunderkinds. Instead we are producing the most anxious generation ever.

Thirty years ago, the notion that children from secure, affluent family units could be so stressed that they were suffering low mood and anxiety disorders would have seemed ridiculous. Now experts are reporting a steep increase in the number of children suffering from depression starting in primary school.

But over that period of time, there has been a complete about-turn in what we believe should be our priorities for our children. Somehow being parents who were around to love and provide food and shelter for our children was no longer enough. Science, global competition, marketing and general anxiety converged to convince us that we had to upgrade our children. Fear of the future has clouded our judgement.

Gradually, babies stopped being allowed to play and discover themselves as they have done for thousands of years. They instead had to be stimulated around the clock to grow better brains. It was no longer acceptable for your child to be average. Now they had to be optimised. In our obsession with proving our worth through our children, we have lost sight of the fact that our own stress and anxiety are the greatest enemies of good parenting – and that our children's stress and anxiety are the biggest obstacles to their achievement.

Children still in nappies are being subjected to academic curricula and assessed for personal development, numeracy and communication in state nurseries before starting formal classes at five, because the government says this will make them more employable. Instead of standing behind them and pointing them in the right direction, we have crossed over into dragging them towards a finish line that never quite comes into view.

It's not nostalgic to point out that times have changed for our children – and our parenting styles have changed accordingly. Our worries for the future mean that instead of accepting them for who they are, we now constantly measure them to assess their chances of success in every area. In the past, parents were content to be raising an 'ordinary' child. Now ordinary has come to mean overlooked.

Within the last few years, it has become no longer enough for our children to be strong in one or two areas. Now it's deemed that a truly successful child has to be an all-rounder in the academic subjects, sport and music. Low-key internal exams to prepare children for the 11-plus, O levels and A levels were also judged not sufficient to keep track. It was decided that children should be graded in public exams at every available opportunity with SATs tests.

The gaps between the exams became shorter as grades became the primary goal. Now, no sooner have children left the GCSE exam hall than they are studying for AS levels a year later. Even A grades have to be liberally sprinkled with stars to really count. University application forms have to read like CVs, in which students must prove to tutors they have been absorbed by their chosen subject since birth, yet still had the time to scale the highest peaks in Britain and do volunteering as part of their Duke of Edinburgh Award. But expecting our children to be good at everything is an unrealistic and unfair burden which makes children feel like they are always falling short, however well they do. However much we try to hide it, they still get the message they are never good enough.

Furthermore, in today's hothouse there are so many more arenas for disappointment than there once were. The confidence of children as young as four is hit hard if they don't make it into the private school their well-off parents want for them. Children in the comprehensive system given SATS in primary are made aware early on if they are not measuring up. As one educational psychologist told me: 'The parents think the children are not aware they are failing, but the children are fully aware. They have a feeling that mummy and daddy are not happy with them.'

Whether in the state or private school system, if we teach children to judge themselves by external standards – what school they go to or what exam results they get – the law of averages means that most of the time, they will feel they are failing.

☆ ☆ ☆

It's not just academic pressures that our children have to contend with. On top of these, a new set of stressors has also started bearing down on them.

Popularity and good looks have always been prized in adolescence. But a generation ago, you were not held up to public humiliation if you did not score highly in these counts. Already plagued by the insecurities of puberty, today's children must find the time to live up to impossibly high ideals of looks and bodily perfection as well as dress themselves according to a red-carpet-ready dress code. If they fail on any count, they risk being publicly slated by their peers on social networks.

The result is that at the same time as British children have become the most tested on Earth, they have also become the most distracted and miserable. UNICEF has put British children in sixteenth place – out of twenty-one countries – for happiness. Data from a Children's Society survey of 30,000 young people aged eight to sixteen suggests that half a million people in that age group are actively unhappy. More than 80,000 primary school children are already estimated to suffer from a severe form of depression.

Experts say that high-stakes testing is contributing to a rise in suicides in young men and self-harm in young women.

In the UK, suicide is the second most common cause of death among fifteen- to nineteen-year-olds after road accidents. The number of children and teenagers who called ChildLine in order to talk about killing themselves more than doubled between 2004 and 2008. At the same time, the charity says the number of children calling about self-harm is soaring at breakneck speed, with a sixty-eight per cent increase year on year in 2012, a rise they attribute to children needing to find a coping mechanism.

Looking to the future, the picture is no rosier. The World Health Organisation has warned that adolescents in the developed world have the fastest-growing incidence of mental health problems on the planet. Furthermore, today's stressed children will turn into the depressed adults of tomorrow.

Girls and boys process this pressure differently. Boys may isolate themselves in technology, and immerse themselves in video games, or internet porn or alcohol. When girls can't identify their feelings, they try to keep up the pretence of perfection and turn their anger in on themselves. They find ways to express pain physically by starving themselves or hurting themselves – because that still feels preferable to the emotional pain they feel inside.

As Lucie Russell, Director of Campaigns at children's mental health charity YoungMinds, points out, our children are living in an 'unprecedentedly toxic climate'. She says: 'Young people today are growing up in a harsh environment with ever-increasing stress to perform at school. Being at school is hard: there is a lot of testing and focus on exams. 'Someone who gets below a C grade can feel like a failure. Job prospects for young people are also awful, and there is an online world where they can be victims of cyber-bullying and they constantly have to think about how to present themselves. There is always pressure to be the perfect person.'

☆ ☆ ☆

I imagine many of you have picked up this book because you genuinely want the best for your child – but you can't see any way of achieving that in the current climate without being a tiger parent. Maybe you have had enough not only of how the relentless pace of modern family life ruins your experience of having children – but also how the constant tension poisons the atmosphere in your home.

Perhaps you have tired of the competitive undercurrents with other parents at the school gates; the conversations which feel like duels;

the icy smiles you have to feign as humblebrags (see page 111) about reading levels, maths scores and music grades rain down on you like body blows. Or possibly you hate the constant, overarching fear that other parents are working harder than you are to make their offspring excel and get ahead of yours?

Most of all, there's a good chance you don't like the way being measured, assessed and judged all the time makes the children you love feel about themselves. Possibly you can't remember the last time you saw your children truly feeling carefree.

So you might want a way out. But you simply can't see an option if your child is not going to be left behind.

As we will find out in the next chapter, our natural concern has been neatly hijacked by big business and tutoring firms who know there's money to be made from panicking parents. This is against a background of persistent assertions that our education system is under attack. Of course there will be plenty of people who say that as the UK and US plummet down the international league table rankings, what we need is *more* pushy parenting, not less. Others will say this is a middle-class issue which only affects a few hotbeds of competitive parenting around the country.

Indeed, it's true that the middle classes are the ones who are passing on the most pressure to their children – because they feel the most under threat. The university places they took for granted now feel at risk from students from other parts of the world, where academic hard work is part of an even deeper-rooted cultural expectation.

But this is about much more than the amusing antics of a few bourgeois families denied bragging rights about having a child at Oxbridge. Seven out of ten people now view themselves as belonging to Middle Britain. The boom in tutoring is not just fuelled by well-off parents trying to get their children into selective private schools. It is also being fed by less affluent families who are also worried about SATs and future employment prospects.

Not all the blame can be conveniently laid at the feet of pushy parents, either, though it may be convenient to scapegoat them as comic, narcissistic slave-drivers living out their dreams through their unfortunate offspring. But just as fierce is the influence of pushy schools and above them pushy education ministers whose main priority is to train up children to be worker bees in an international workforce.

But there is also an uncomfortable truth lurking here. The children of the most over-invested, overambitious generation of parents in history are being educated alongside those from some of the most under-invested and economically deprived families – and treated by governments as if there is a one-size-fits-all solution. At the same time as our newspapers obsess about the latest extreme of tiger parents, there are also shock-horror headlines about children turning up at nurseries barely able to speak, huge swathes of six-year-olds unable to read basic words, and school-leavers still not meeting the standards of Maths and English required by employers.

The underlying reasons for this low achievement are often that these children are products of extreme poverty, teenage pregnancies, households in which English is not yet spoken or chaotic family backgrounds. But the measures introduced to catch the so-called 'tail' – like nappy curricula, early nursery-school starts and SATS throughout primary – also end up frying children who have been overcooked from the start.

At one end of the scale, high-stakes testing is turbo-charging an elite class of alpha children who have been on the hamster wheel from the moment of birth. At the other, it is alienating a generation of children who have been branded as failures early on because they never got the same level of parental investment. Because children see the world in black and white terms, it feels like a case of all-or-nothing. They don't have the experience to know there is a middle ground, so they give up.

The result is a two-tier education system with a huge achievement gap into which more children are falling all the time.

☆ ☆ ☆

The other possibility is that you are reading this book to see if you are a tiger parent – and how you stack up compared to other parents. After all, millions of parents around the world read Amy Chua's *Battle Hymn of the Tiger Mother*, not because they wanted to throw in the towel on pushy parenting, but because they wanted to see if it really worked or to justify their own methods. If so, you may already be of the opinion that the world is a competitive place and if your children are to do well, they had just better get used to it. You may also believe that 'healthy competition' makes children try harder and do their best.

Maybe you feel emboldened by the fact that you believe your efforts are paying off and secretly feel that any parent who opts out is not prepared to put in the work it requires.

But this is not a book that puts free-range parenting in one corner and competitive parenting in another. Nor does it recommend a return to the 'everyone must have prizes' practices of the 1980s.

Absolutely, as parents, we must help children reach their potential. But our expectations must be fair, reasonable and healthy, based on their individual strengths. They must be built around what *they need*, not what *we want*.

Our expectations should not be set by the standards of schools intent on boosting their reputations on league tables – or the economic goals of governments aiming to turn our offspring into foot soldiers to compete with economic rivals in the Far East with entirely different values.

As their first guardians, it's up to parents to speak up about the effects this pressure is having on the commodities in this system: our children. It's up to us to ask some other far-reaching questions that politicians, looking at economic forecasts, won't be interested in.

Has competition actually been proven to make children do their best? Or because we live in a consumerist society, do we just assume it does? What lesson is the 'every man for himself' mentality giving the next generation? Does the world really need young people who view every other member of their peer group as a potential rival?

At a time when the world faces issues that demand global cooperation, such as climate change, over-population and economic collapse, are these really the values we need to be enshrining for the future?

☆ ☆ ☆

This book will present the latest research from all over the world about how the competitive society is changing childhood. From Japan to China to Finland, it will look at how different approaches to achievement in those cultures have affected parents – and children too. It will examine how modern parents came to believe that life is a race and that they are almost solely responsible for the success of their child.

Taming the Tiger Parent grew out of my last book, in which I looked at the damage being done to children's well-being by sexualisation. When *Where Has My Little Girl Gone?* was published in 2011, I was one of a number of voices starting to raise concerns about the effects of pornography on children's mental health.

At first, such worries were dismissed by some as a prudish moral panic. But then the effects started to filter down to the behaviour of children. Now those who work with children say there is little doubt that porn has led to a distorted view of sex and a rise in sexual bullying, violence and expectation among the young.

This book arose out of the last because I believe that the pressures bearing down on our young people are just as great a threat to their mental health. Our children are in a vulnerable position because at the same time as we load so much on to them, we have starved them of the resources they need to stay strong. By depriving kids of the experiences that create resilience and emotional balance, our schools and homes have become fertile ground for our children to develop depression, anxiety, self-harming tendencies and eating disorders.

At the same time, we need to redefine pushy parenting – because it's undeniable that children will do better if they are supported and encouraged to reach their potential. There is no doubt that involved, interested parents can make a huge difference to a child – as long as they respect that child's individual strengths and talents.

But instead of being ringmasters cracking the whip to get our children to perform better, we need to reconsider our roles in this system. Instead of taking away the seats in this frantic game of musical chairs we make our children play, we need to offer our children more choice. Instead of turning our homes into hothouses, we need to turn them into havens.

As parents we must walk a difficult tightrope. How do we tread the line between supporting our children and stifling them? Where is the boundary between stretching them and stressing them?

This book is more than an analysis of what is going wrong for our children – it also offers practical solutions. In this sink-or-swim environment, it's easy to assume that pushy parenting is the life-jacket required to keep our children's heads above water. It can be painful too to know that what we have done out of love may also have caused harm. As parents it's our natural instinct to protect, but sometimes we get too close – and care too much – to see the bigger picture.

Like a jab, the realisation of how you have been influenced may prick your conscience at first, as it did with mine. But by analysing the pressures on yourselves and your children, you will be inoculating your children against them.

The first part of the book analyses how we arrived at this state of affairs; the second looks at how it affects our children. The third part looks at how to put our children's well-being first – and help them survive in a competitive world. It also looks at what to do if your child has already been damaged.

Please note that as far as possible I refer to tiger parents, not just tiger mothers. In my experience, helicopter parenting – or constantly hovering over every piece of schoolwork or extra-curricular activity – is not just the preserve of women. Until now, fathers have got off remarkably lightly. These days, both parents are actively involved in the push – and fathers are just as likely to be standing at the back of a violin concert, doing the air-bowing.

This book asks you to examine what you mean by being a successful parent. Should we judge ourselves on our ability to turn our offspring into high-achievers who gain entry to the top universities and get the best jobs in order to buy nice houses, holidays and expensive cars?

Or should we judge ourselves on the ability to guide our children towards becoming happy, ethical, compassionate people who like themselves and who value the world around them?

Of course, put like this, it's a no-brainer. My question is why are we still raising children as if we don't know the answer?

PART ONE

HOW TIGER PARENTING BECAME A GLOBAL FORCE

'Up until the 1950s, we placed the needs of children ahead of the needs of parents, and children flourished. From the 50s on, we have put the needs of children and adolescents beneath the needs of adults and parents. The outcome is a lot of stress.'

Dr David Elkind, Emeritus Professor of Child Development

'One from a mother whose child was in utero…she was convinced that her child was going to be gifted.'

Hal Curties, the vice-principal of a school for exceptional children, who receives a lot of early applications for places at his school

THE HISTORY OF PUSHY PARENTING

AROUND 100 YEARS AGO, an agony aunt by the name of Florence Stacpoole had some bracing advice for a mother who wanted to know how much time to spend entertaining her baby. 'Babies under six months should never be played with,' she replied briskly in her answer in Mother and Home magazine. 'The less of it at any time, the better for the infant.'

'Doctors say they are made nervous and irritable…' she added, for good measure. 'The brain grows almost as much during the first year as during the rest of the life. You can understand then why quiet is necessary for babies under a year old.'

This verbal bucket of cold water shows it's not just agony aunt advice that has changed since 1915. Parenting trends have too. For tens of thousands of years, parents never gave a second thought to the development of their infants. The young in a community were left to learn through play and imitation of grown-ups.

So what happened in the intervening century to persuade us that far from leaving our children in peace, we need to stimulate them every waking moment – and that ninety-nine per cent of their success in life rests on the quality and quantity of this input?

True, there had been some sporadic attempts at pushiness before today's tiger parenting trend took hold. Wolfgang Amadeus Mozart was famously fêted as a child genius when he was wheeled around the courts of Europe by his ambitious father Leopold at the age of seven in the 1760s. But a few years later when Johann, the father of Ludwig van Beethoven, attempted to create the same level of interest in his son, he failed and became a laughing stock.

For most of history, precocious children were viewed as oddities – like circus sideshow acts – and with some suspicion. The general view was that children arrived on the Earth as uncivilised savages and it was the job of adults to discipline the undesirable qualities out of them. If your child was not blessed with looks or intellect, that was judged to be 'unfortunate', but more down to the will of God than anything else.

There was the Jesuit phrase 'Give me the child up to the age of seven and I will give you the man.' But this was a reference to a child's moral character, not his future earning power. If parents did have a role in shaping children, it wasn't to push them. It was to punish. The adults in a family saw their main job as instilling self-restraint, good manners and citizenship. There was little quibbling about careers. Sons generally followed their fathers into their professions. Girls were trained by their mothers in whatever skills they needed.

Although it was John Locke, the seventeenth-century philosopher, who first came up with the idea of the child as a blank slate waiting to be written on, he also believed that children first needed to be taught a strong framework of moral values. Only then were they ready to learn addition and subtraction.

As the middle class emerged in Georgian England, parents were mainly concerned with teaching character and refinement, Mrs Bennet style, to make girls more marriageable. Too much education was considered a dangerous thing for women, in case it distracted them from the practical business of running a household.

Learning was seen to get in the way. Agony aunt letters of the time included complaints that husbands were less enchanted by their brides' love of poetry, and more interested in whether the fires were lit and there was supper on the table. Women were tersely reminded that 'Your first duty *now* is to your husband. No wife should have a soul above buttons (which means above sewing them on). Nor should she ignore the fact that man's heart lies very near his stomach.'

At the same time infancy began to be cherished, particularly among the upper classes, who did not have to set their children to work. Thanks to the dewy-eyed portraits of Joshua Reynolds and Thomas Gainsborough, children started to be seen as distinct beings that parents could show off for their angelic beauty.

By the 1840s, the invention of the pram was allowing pigeon-chested mamas to parade their babies in public. Plenty of air and exercise were considered prerequisites for successfully raising a child. A rosy cheek or a chubby leg was more likely to be admired than early language skills. Most middle-class children were educated at home by governesses – and so there was rarely the chance for parents to compare their children. If a boy showed particular intellectual curiosity, a well-to-do family might send him off to boarding school to develop character.

At best, most ordinary working-class children might have attended Sunday school. In 1870, the Victorian government introduced weekday schooling for five- to ten-year-olds. But there was not universal enthusiasm for the idea. Child labour was one of the driving forces of the Industrial Revolution. Working-class youngsters were considered such valuable workers that many parents preferred to keep them out of school so they could continue to earn an income for the family.

Nor did classrooms seem very inviting propositions. Children who did not shine were shamed with dunce hats, beatings and banishment to cobwebbed corners. Failure to learn was seen as a fault of character as much as intellect – and often branded as laziness.

At the turn of the century, a new sort of book also began to hit the shelves. As populations were made up of fewer extended families and more, smaller self-contained units, bourgeois mothers sought advice in the form of child-rearing manuals. Mainly written by male doctors, one of the most influential was *Feeding and Care of Baby* by Frederic Truby King, published in 1913, which dictated the way women reared children right up until the Second World War. Still, the advice was to stay hands-off as much as possible. Children would gradually grow into themselves. An infant should be treated like 'an independent puppy playing in the yard'. The idea of toys was scoffed at. Instead Truby King declared an infant's 'earliest play should be mainly with his first playmate – himself – his own feet'.

Like Stacpoole, Truby King advocated 'quiet and peaceful surroundings' for 'the rapid growth of the brain'. The message was clear: babies should be fed and cared for and kept safe, but otherwise left to their own devices. But around the same time, there was the first official sighting of the pushy mother in the form of the classic 'stage mother'. The rapid building of theatres and the music halls of the late Victorian period meant an explosion of roles for children.

Parents started to view their offspring's singing and dancing talents as a lucrative source of income. In 1911 the world's first stage school, the Italia Conti Academy, was established in London. One of the pupils was the young Noël Coward, whose withering indictment of mothers living out their dreams through their children was immortalised in his song 'Don't Put Your Daughter On The Stage, Mrs Worthington'. Indeed his own ambitious mother, Violet, had put Noël there at the age of twelve.

Gradually, the Victorian idea that children should be seen and not heard started to give way to a more novel view of the child as a sensitive, vulnerable soul. Far from having nothing to do with how their children's personalities were formed, psychoanalyst Sigmund Freud ventured that almost the entire responsibility for children's happiness lay at their parents' feet.

Children began to be viewed more as a different species in their own right who thought and saw the world in an entirely different way. At first, studies of child psychology focused on disturbed or mentally ill children. But gradually even ordinary children came to be seen as fascinating, complicated creatures whose learning was worthy of academic study.

In previous centuries, as few as half of all children had been expected to reach adulthood. Now that advances in medicine meant that parents did not have to worry as much about their offspring's physical health, adults started focusing on their mental well-being instead. They became invested in the idea of giving their children 'happy childhoods'. Child-rearing began to be seen as more of a transaction. The more you put in as a parent, the better your child was likely to turn out.

Amid all this research, it was Swiss developmental psychologist Jean Piaget who made the most impact, with his theories on the basic stages of a child's intellectual growth. According to his ideas, children could be viewed as 'little scientists', just as intelligent as adults in their own way.

As the twentieth century wore on, there was a shift in the perception of the importance of children as society became more fluid. Social hierarchies started to break down. Contraception meant couples had fewer children, who they tended to value and invest in them more.

Status and wealth were no longer necessarily inherited. The decline of manual labour and agriculture meant a child ultimately needed a career. If they passed the 11-plus and became a successful professional, they could take a step up the class ladder.

Education rapidly became seen as the key to improving one's lot in life. Exams started to decide the course of a child's future. Schooling became standardised. The introduction of O and A levels in the 1950s meant that, for the first time, children's achievements could be directly compared. Sport became organised, leading to more competition. Schools became larger, creating more intense peer pressure – not only between children, but between their parents too.

Within schools, youngsters were generally left to develop at their own pace. Children were seen to arrive in the world with their own intellectual capabilities – they were either 'brainy' or 'thick', with 'average' in between. But parents did not consider that they could do much to influence their child's brain power. It was considered enough to 'rear' your children by feeding, housing and teaching them some manners. Education was considered best left to schools.

Hitler's creation of the Hitler Youth was one of the first sinister indicators that adults had started to recognise the importance of sculpting the next generation – and how they could be manipulated en masse.

SHARPEN YOUR CLAWS

HOW PUSHY PARENTS TURN INTO TIGERS

WHEN I BROUGHT MY first school report home in the summer of 1971, while I am sure my mother was pleased to read 'Tanith is reading well for her age', I'm also certain she didn't take the credit for it.

So what happened in the intervening thirty-five years to make me feel so different when, with trembling hands, I opened my daughter's first school report? How, like millions of other parents, had I also come to believe that it was up to me whether or not my child excelled?

Furthermore, how had child psychologist Donald Winnicott's concept of the 'good enough mother' in the 1950s – a parent who does enough by simply tending to her child with love, patience and care – morphed so quickly into the tiger parent whose job is never done until her child is the best?

In fact, by the time I had started school, the baby education bandwagon was already rolling. Three years before I was born, it had been set in motion by an American physical therapist called Glenn Doman. In 1963, he published a book called *Teach Your Baby To Read*. Based on the rehabilitation of brain-injured children, Doman's central theory rested on his observation that an infant's brain grows more in size in the first year than at any other time in life. This translated, in his mind, to the fact that the organ needed to be stimulated as much as possible until growth slowed down at the age of three.

Babies arrived in the world so thirsty for knowledge that Doman went so far as to propose that they would rather learn than eat – and that toys were invented by adults to distract young children from what they *really* wanted to do – which was to get more intelligent.

For the next twenty years, Doman, an avuncular figure with a snow-white Colonel Sanders-style beard, preached his theories round the clock on US TV on infomercials from his headquarters, The Institutes for the Achievement of Human Potential, outside Philadelphia. However questionable his reading of the science was, his message that all babies were intellectuals on a par with Leonardo da Vinci - if only we adults were prepared to help unlock their genius – proved irresistible to parents, as was his favourite phrase, 'Mom is the best teacher'.

From the start, few experts in child development supported Doman's claims that babies could actually read. An infant might recognise the shapes of distinctive-looking words, such as 'eye' or 'spaghetti', and give the illusion of correctly recognising the right flashcard. But most infants were still more interested in chewing them. It was pointed out that an intelligent dog could also be trained to do the same thing.

But already, it was too late. In the craze for self-improvement that pervaded the 1970s and 1980s, parents had already enthusiastically seized on the theory that they could give their child a head start which would last them through life.

Linda Hale, then 38, was among the suburban mums who became Doman's disciples. For taking a $490 course and giving her nine-week-old son Kevin daily maths and reading flashcard sessions, she was awarded her 'professional mothering certificate'. Even thirty years ago – in 1983 – her reasons for taking the course provide a telling glimpse of the growing neurosis that was starting to consume parenting. 'There's so much pressure to get into college,' Linda told *Newsweek* magazine. 'You have to start them young and push them on toward their goal. They have to be aware of everything – the alphabet, numbers, reading. I want to fill these little sponges as much as possible.'

In the same article there were also worrying signs that the importance of raising a happy, well-adjusted child was slowly losing ground to the idea that it was more important to raise a successful one. The new ABCs of babyhood, *Newsweek* added, were 'Anxiety, Betterment and Competition'.

At the same time, parents started to feel besieged by countless competing theories on the best way to bring up a child. Bottle or breast? Co-sleeping or controlled crying? Until then, baby boomer parents raising their kids in the 1950s and 1960s assumed that, behind closed doors, most parents were raising their children the same way as them. Now every parent was following a different theory about how to do it best.

On top of being told that raising a child was the most important job any adult would ever do, the next generation of parents were no longer even sure how it was supposed to be done.

As part of the quest for certainty, Doman's ideas filled a void. *Teach Your Baby To Read* sold five million copies and was translated into more than twenty languages.

It didn't take long for the first side-effects of hothousing to surface. 'I see an enormous amount of pressure on children,' paediatrician Paul Batalden complained in the early eighties. 'It shows up in headaches and abdominal pain. Parents come into my office complaining their child looks peaked or is tired all the time or doesn't feel excited about living any more.'

Other psychologists started coming forward to report treating distressed and overstressed two- and three-year-olds who were pulling out their hair in clumps and ripping out their eyelashes. In a message which fell on deaf ears, psychiatrist Angelica Frias sounded this ominous note of caution: 'A baby can always learn cognitive skills. But it's very difficult to go back and redo emotional development.' Another warned: 'Other signs of disturbance may not surface for years.' Even the kindly oracle of twentieth-century child-rearing Dr Benjamin Spock stepped forward to say that he was worried that babies were being 'over-intellectualised'.

EXPLOITING THE INSECURITY OF MIDDLE-CLASS PARENTS

WHILE DOMAN NEVER SUCCEEDED in creating a generation of early readers – US literacy rates are now among the lowest in the world – he did prove another point. He demonstrated that the insecurity of middle-class parents could be turned into cold, hard cash.

Even if some parents weren't entirely sure that they could make their children smarter, most figured it was worth a try. What if the books, news reports and toy manufacturers had got it right – and little Johnnie's failure to get into Harvard in years to come could be put down to the fact that mum and dad hadn't properly wired up his brain during babyhood? They would never forgive themselves.

Now the early education bandwagon was accelerating at breakneck speed, it seemed to matter less and less what the actual science said. When psychologist Anthony DeCasper carried out seminal experiments which seemed to show that babies recognise their mothers' voices in the womb, marketers quickly got in on the act. The result was the PREGAPHONE, a sort of oversized stethoscope, which promised to enable mothers to communicate with their babies and make them more intelligent. No matter that DeCasper said that simply hearing the mother's voice was enough for the foetus and that too much noise could damage a baby's hearing later in pregnancy. Or that neurologists pointed out that there were good reasons why wombs are dark and quiet: mainly that before birth babies sleep ninety per cent of the time.

The latest parenting books no longer focused on the basics of feeding and caring for a baby, as they had in the past. Now they concentrated on raising IQ instead – with one bestseller, *How To Have A Smarter Baby*, modestly promising an increase of up to thirty points.

As the claims became increasingly outlandish, so did the protests of the researchers who pointed out that marketers were confusing neurology – the study of the cell structure of the brain – with psychology. True, a child's development did benefit from a loving, nurturing relationship with its caregivers. The experience of the children left in Romanian orphanages showed that little ones left in isolation and without human contact did suffer huge cognitive setbacks which could never be completely overcome. But the scientists pointed out that this was not the same as asserting that if you never left a child alone for a moment, its intelligence would grow incrementally.

By the year 2000, the term 'baby burn-out' had been coined to describe the fretful, wired behaviour of infants who could not settle because they had been overstimulated. Instead of promoting a love of literature, Professor David Elkind, America's foremost professor of child development, also stepped forward to say that he believed that one-half of all literacy problems were due to children being pushed to read before they were ready. He added that studies showed that youngsters introduced to books later were more spontaneous, eager readers than those shown flashcards in the cradle.

Even harder to evaluate, Elkind pointed out, was the impact of the disappointed look on a parent's face when, after two years of flashcards, a child was barely reading *The Cat in the Hat* on their own, let alone *War and Peace*. But as history will show, a theory as seductive as 'parents are the masters of their children's intelligence' doesn't go away that easily.

CREATING YOUR BABY EINSTEIN

S O, IT WAS IN this atmosphere that I plonked my first baby in her bouncy seat in front of a Baby Einstein video. There I left her to gaze up at a surreal mix of lava lamps, wind-up toys and glove puppets dancing to xylophone reductions of Mozart's greatest hits. Common sense should have told me this was unlikely to do anything but confuse her or send her to sleep. But just in case I was in any doubt, ad pitches such as 'Great Minds Start Little' and 'A Little Genius in the Making' overcame my misgivings fairly easily. It also helped that I could pop the baby in front of the TV for a guilt-free half-hour while I caught up with doing stuff around the house.

Baby Einstein was the brainchild of Julie Aigner-Clark, a Colorado schoolteacher who filmed her first video on a borrowed camera in her basement in 1997. Einstein may have cracked relativity, but Aigner-Clark's brilliance was merging the prevailing idea that babies were wannabe prodigies with the recent discovery of the Mozart Effect – a study which claimed that university students who listened to ten minutes of the composer's music scored slightly better in tests.

Aigner-Clark's timing was flawless. Baby Einstein was launched into a waiting world where there had never been so much interest in upgrading children. Here was the parents' obsession that they should do more to stimulate their babies neatly turned into a convenient product and sold straight back to them. Governor Zell Miller of Georgia was such a fan he advocated sending classical music tapes to the parent of every newborn in the state when they left hospital. Soon Florida had passed its own 'Beethoven Babies Bill' requiring all state-run baby-care facilities to play at least one symphony to their charges every day. Similar ideas were introduced in Tennessee and Colorado.

Within five years, one in four US families had bought at least one educational baby video. By 2001, Baby Einstein had racked up sales of $21 million and the company was sold to Disney. It was such a success that President Bush praised it in his 2007 State of the Union address as summing up 'the great enterprising spirit of America'.

However, there were some problems on the horizon. Scientists trying to replicate the experiments that the Mozart Effect theory was based on came out saying that they could find no such results. More damaging to Baby Einstein was the fact that some studies started to suggest that far from improving baby's abilities, educational videos might even thwart them. A University of Washington research team, which surveyed 1,000 families in 2006, found that babies between 8 and 16 months who regularly watched brainy baby videos knew seventeen per cent fewer words than those who never saw them. The methodology was queried but nevertheless a complaint was filed with the Federal Trade Commission alleging that the firm had engaged in false and deceptive advertising. None of this was helped by the timing of an announcement by the American Academy of Pediatrics that babies and toddlers under two should get no screen time at all.

As the criticism mounted, Disney raised the white flag, offered parents refunds and downgraded their sales pitch. But not before Baby Einstein claimed parents had misunderstood their mission statement all along. 'We've never claimed they're educational,' said a company spokesman. No, apparently the goal all along had been to 'instil in infants a love of classical music and art and nature'.

CHILD'S PLAY

THE RISE OF THE EDUCATIONAL TOY

EVEN TODAY YOU COULD take a trip down the aisles of Britain's largest toy retailer, Toys R Us, and still believe that it's never too early to get your baby ready for algebra. You only have to look down the side of a box containing the Fisher Price Learning Table to see the impressive array of skills your baby *might* acquire by playing with the product: alphabet, numbers, colours, shapes, words, opposites, actions, textures and manners, to name just a few.

Here is the Mozart Effect gone mad. Newborns who don't even know their feet belong to them are encouraged to make music by kicking giant piano keys in infant play gyms. Most of the toys in the educational aisle are so hectic as to be migraine inducing. Pity the poor infant who has left a warm, dark womb to be assaulted by this riot of pop-up plastic, noise and colour.

Not content to wait for school, parents can even get report cards on how well their babies and toddlers are doing. If you buy Leapfrog toys – the very name implies your tot will vault over their peers – you can connect to a spreadsheet which tracks their skills and 'helps you recognise where your child excels and areas where he/she may need more support'.

The packaging is careful enough – after recent experiences in the US – not to explicitly promise to make your child brainier. Instead, as if by pure coincidence, and apropos of nothing in particular, boxes just happen to be plastered with nuggets such as 'The ability to detect patterns helps with later algebraic reasoning'.

The educational spiel may be long-winded but the message is clear. Toys are no longer toys. They are teachers. In this fast-tracked world, even something as simple as a skipping rope comes with flashing lights in order to teach the times tables, which can then be tested in 'target mode'.

High-tech as these toys are, looking into the future you have to wonder how they will fare against the march of the i-toy. Increasingly playthings are becoming accessories to fit around tablet technology, loaded up with educational apps. There is the iBounce, a trampoline fitted with an iPad holder, and the iTeddy – a cuddly toy to hold an iPad in place. There is even an iPotty so your child can play with apps while learning to use their bowels. Baby gyms for newborns also come with a slot so they can stare up at your iPhone. No wonder there is now the term 'iPaddy' to describe the tantrum a child has when their tablet computer is taken away.

But what all these toys have in common is what marketers call 'an acceptability halo'. Parents like them because they keep children occupied – and they might even make them better at school too. They have found a captive market with couples who, through marrying later and being brought up in smaller families, have little experience with babies, and aren't at all sure how to play with them. The fact that these toys promise parents to teach their infants as well as free the adults up to answer an email or a text message is also useful.

Even thinking generously, most neuroscientists say our expectations of educational toys and videos are overstated at best – and unfounded at worst. In translating the science from lab to nursery, the message has got seriously muddled. Like any 'next big thing', a grain of truth has been taken and magnified into a money-spinner.

It's not just the fact that educational toys don't help. A growing number of experts are taking the view that they actively deprive children of the time and brain space they need to learn more vital skills, like open-ended and imaginary play. While it's true that leaving a child in a darkened room with no stimulation means it won't develop as many brain connections, the flipside is not that the more you expose the cleverer they will be. There is a limit to how much the brain can process and absorb, say the neuroscientists. Like a sponge, it can only hold so much.

Take vocabulary – a hot topic because of the comparisons between the number of words used by children from middle-class and deprived backgrounds when they start school. There is no doubt that a child will know more words if they have lots of one-on-one interaction with caregivers who talk to them, rather than being strapped into a pram with an iPhone to play with. But no matter how many words you spout to them, some children have a genetic blueprint which enables them to integrate words more quickly and seamlessly into their speech than others.

Far from helping, brain researchers like the late Professor Peter Huttenlocher believed that the push for early learning could slow down development through neurological 'crowding'. In other words, a glut of information jams the synapses, which would be better used by more creative tasks.

Brain researcher Kathy Hirsh-Pasek says on the subject: 'Imagine that you're waiting for tickets at a movie theatre and there are two lines. Now imagine the manager comes out and closes one of the lines. Your line becomes more crowded, and it takes longer to buy your ticket. So too with neurological crowding.'

Overload a baby and they may also just tune you out. Seven- and eight-month-old babies have also been found to filter out information they find too complicated so that they can focus only on what they are ready for. In one experiment, researchers showed babies images to see which ones they were most interested in. When the pictures got too predictable, the babies got bored. But when the infants were shown 'surprising' images they were not more intrigued. They just switched off.

One of the study's authors, Richard Aslin, a professor of brain and cognitive sciences, said: 'It's like if you tried to teach a six-year-old calculus, they would just have no idea what you're talking about, it would be way too complicated…They focus in on what they can handle and filter out the rest.'

And that's not to mention the hundreds of hours parents spend working to pay for these toys, time which would be better spent directly talking, singing and playing with their infants – which is what the research says, conclusively, *does* make the difference.

Lead author of the study, Professor Celeste Kidd, believes that children learn best from human interaction rather than from the latest gadgets. She said: 'Parents don't need to buy fancy toys to help their children learn. They make the best use of their environment. They are going to look around for what fits their attention level.'

Neuroscientist Dr Lise Eliot, who has spent years studying the infant brain, also believes there is a limit to how much stimulation we should expose our children to. 'Too many toys, activities and outings can create confusion and actually work to a child's detriment, hampering his ability to focus…Whether a room contains three toys or thirty makes little difference in a young child's play but an enormous difference in the level of confusion he has to sort through. Children are usually pretty good at telling us when they're bored but not when they are being overstimulated. Their behaviour, such as fussiness and acting out is often the only sign.'

Brain scientist and molecular biologist John Medina agrees: 'Sadly, myths rush in when facts are few and have a way of snaring people. Even after all these years, many of the products are still out there like untethered gill nets, trapping unsuspecting parents into parting with their hard-earned [cash].' Making learning and playtime stressful is counterproductive, says Medina. 'The more stress hormones swarm their brains, the less likely they are to succeed intellectually.'

Yet fifty years after the publication of Doman's book, the myths it created are still being perpetuated. It has been estimated that there are 48,000 developers globally working on apps for smartphones and tablets to teach young children to speak words, play educational games and speak foreign languages. But when recently asked by consumer groups in the US to provide the evidence that these apps make children cleverer, answer came there none from the toy industry's trade body.

As Medina says: 'The greatest pediatric brain-boosting technology in the world is probably a plain cardboard box, a fresh box of crayons and two hours.' Imagine the money parents would save – and the anxiety we would save the next generation – if we really believed it.

NATURE VERSUS NURTURE

CAN WE 'CREATE' OUR CHILDREN?

TWO YEARS AGO, I sent off a three-inch test tube of saliva – belonging to me, my husband and my two daughters – to be genetically tested.

It was simple. All we had to do was work up enough spit to fill the vial, seal it up and dispatch it to a consumer testing service called 23andMe in California. There, all the DNA in our samples was isolated and processed, and our genetic code was stored on a computer and run up against thousands of research studies isolating the meanings of different genes.

Six weeks later, I got an email announcing that the results had arrived. With some trepidation I logged in, wondering what sort of Pandora's Box I was opening.

The first bit was reassuring. There were no life-altering shocks. Our DNA profiles were compared with half a million other random people around the world. From our results, there was clearly no chance my children had been switched at birth at the hospital or that Anthony was not their father (although naturally this came as no surprise.)

Out of everyone on the database, my daughters had fifty per cent each of our DNA. Even though they have completely different looks and temperaments, the girls were also found to be eighty-eight per cent alike with each other, making them compatible enough to be organ donors.

Surfing my genome for the 240 traits over the next hour or two was both entertaining and scary. It was fun to find out there was a good reason for my life-long aversion to sprouts: I have a gene that allows me to taste the bitterness in vegetables. On the other hand it was terrifying to find out that I might have an 18.3 per cent genetic risk of developing breast cancer.

Yet as I scrolled down, it was the results for intelligence and temperament which surprised me most. After all, I was part of the generation that believed we were solely responsible for teaching our children to be successful. But hold on a moment. Here on the list were markers for reading ability, measures of intelligence, the capacity to avoid mistakes and even whether breastfeeding my children would have enhanced their IQ.

Of course, this was all really only the entertaining dipping-of-a-toe into a vast ocean. For one thing, there are around ten million SNPs (single-nucleotide polymorphisms) in the human genome, which account for genetic differences between us all. Our reports had looked at just over half a million.

While it was far from being the whole picture, it was clear that a lot more than I realised had been decided on the night of conception. I was being confronted with a slightly different view of the world: that both my children – while being half me and half my husband – came into the world with a strong genetic blueprint that was all their own.

Until recently, *Gattaca*-like visions of the future have made it uncomfortable to suggest that our genes are responsible for intelligence. For years, a debate has raged over whether our children are a product of nature or nurture. But the more science there is, the more it looks as if DNA plays a big role.

Studies of twins – or genetic clones – are showing that even those who had been separated at birth turn out to have remarkably similar personalities and IQ levels. On the other hand, the temperaments and intelligence levels of siblings of different parentage adopted by the same families were not alike at all. In other words, if your biological child was taken away from you at birth and grew up in another family, they wouldn't turn out to be that much different than if you had raised them yourself.

Some of the estimates of how much DNA contributes vary. But on average, studies of twins have come to the conclusion that genes contribute about fifty per cent to a child's intelligence. Beyond this, as scientists map more of the human genome, they are also arriving at the conclusion that the temperamental traits, which mean the difference between a high-flyer and a low-achiever, are also inherited.

Genes, for example, could explain why some children never perform well in exams while others sail through. A study in Taiwan of 779 students taking high-stakes tests found that those who had a particular variant of the COMT gene – which helps regulate the mood-altering chemical dopamine in the brain – got better scores. Their brain coped with exam stress better so they could concentrate better on giving the right answers.

To put it another way, just because you stormed your A levels, you can't automatically assume your child will. Your partner, who is contributing half of their DNA to your child's make-up – may pass on the other version of the gene which makes them more likely to wilt under exam pressure.

One more piece of DNA may help to explain why some children respond to tiger parenting better than others. A study looked at the influence of a gene called 5-HTT which affects how well the brain uses serotonin, a chemical critical to creating the happy and relaxed state children need in which to learn. Researchers at the University of Denver found that children with two short versions – around twenty per cent of those tested – are born with more difficult temperaments, and they need warmer and more responsive parenting if they are to stay calm and thrive. This has been interpreted to mean that the more these children are pressured, the more negative they will feel and the less likely they are to do well.

True, bright parents are more likely to have bright children. But it is estimated there are thousands of different genes which fit together like a mosaic to make up the bigger picture of our intellectual abilities. Also acting on these are DNA instructions for how kids handle stress and what kind of temperament they have – both of which will govern how they apply that intelligence.

LETTING GO OF THE FANTASY OF WHAT OUR CHILDREN ARE SUPPOSED TO BE

IT WAS WHILE I was researching this book that I heard a story about a man who is one of Britain's leading thinkers. One of his three children needed some help because her schoolwork was not going as well as might have been expected, so he took her to a tutor to be assessed.

As he watched the teacher cough and splutter her way through the none-too-pleasing news that his child was not in the same academic top drawer as he was, he interrupted her to put her out of misery. 'It's OK, I understand,' he said reassuringly. 'It's regression to the mean.' In other words, he accepted what many other parents prefer to deny. Just because you and your partner are high-flyers doesn't make you more likely to produce an über-baby. It could even make you less likely.

Genetics experts like Dr Stephen Hsu of Michigan State University, who studies how we inherit intelligence, says that if two parents have an IQ of 160, the statistical reversion makes them most likely to produce a child with an IQ of 136. There is only a small percentage chance that their offspring would exceed 160. For two parents with an IQ of 145, the mean would be 127, with a less than ten per cent chance the child would beat their mother and father's scores.

After all, if there were no regression to the mean, cleverer people, who tend to marry people in the same intellectual bracket, would be breeding a race of super-geniuses. While the human race may be getting a little brighter – by about three IQ points a decade – most of that rise is considered to be down to better nutrition, exposure to a wider range of experiences and also more practice in taking tests.

The genetics of intelligence can also be thought of like height. Having tall or short parents is usually a very good predictor of how tall you will be – but not always. 'Regression to the mean implies that even if two giants or two geniuses were to marry, the children would not, on average, be giants or geniuses,' says Dr Hsu. 'On the positive side, it means that below-average parents typically produce offspring that are closer to average.'

None of this is surprising to animal breeders, he adds. 'They know all this. They are using stuff to actually get where they want to go. It's only controversial because people are involved and people don't like the conclusions the science is leading them to.' But anyone who's had more than one child gradually gets the picture that children arrive in the world with their own individual strengths and weaknesses. To a certain extent the dice have already been rolled.

In order to accept both how random and unpredictable the act of passing on our genes to our children is, consider how our kids inherit looks. Take two of the best-looking people in the world – Angelina Jolie and Brad Pitt would be obvious examples. While there is no doubt that the three biologically born Jolie-Pitt children are likely to be very attractive, and look like their parents, it's doubtful all three will be better-looking.

My point is this: as parents it's wise to let go of the fantasy of what our children are 'supposed to be'. When our sons and daughters come into the world, we immediately assume they are as clever as us, and it's up to us to make them even brighter. But children can be damaged beyond repair if they are expected to live up to standards they can't meet. Of course we can spot and make the most of their potential. There is also growing evidence that shows that the environment can act on the way certain genes work.

But if our children still aren't sailing into Mensa and our dis-appointment comes through as exasperation, irritation and impatience, this can be highly corrosive to a child's self-worth, especially if your child is one of the more sensitive ones. Every infant comes into the world with a unique set of strengths and challenges. The secret to happy children and happy parents is how to deal with the spin of the genetic wheel – which was set in motion the night they were conceived.

THE RISE OF THE TUTOR

IN A FACELESS OFFICE block in a North London suburb, a high-level business meeting is taking place. Around a giant boardroom table, there are six potential investors, all keen to put money into one of the biggest business boom areas around – tutoring.

As a power-dressed Kumon executive scrolls through a Powerpoint presentation, the talk is of branding, business models and big returns. In return for a £3,000 investment, we are told that a client base of 150 children could earn franchisees an annual income of around £70,000 a year. With 500 students on the roster, profits would approach a cool quarter of a million.

The Kumon method was invented in 1954 by an anxious father called Toru Kumon, who was looking for a way for his son to catch up when he got a bad mark in a maths test. Since then, it's been a business built on an inexhaustible global resource: parental panic. The Kumon executive puts it even more succinctly: 'It plugs into the fear: "Why is my neighbour's child doing better than mine?" That completely natural reaction…still exists in parents today.'

Indeed. If there was a gust of paranoia in 1954, it's been whipped into a full-scale hurricane now. Year on year, growth is twelve per cent. In the UK alone, Kumon tutors 70,000 pupils, and it has four million students across the world. To complete this happy picture of ongoing success and upward profit, the walls of the Kumon UK offices are decorated with countless pictures of beaming children, pencils poised over maths questions.

From these, you could easily get the impression that nothing is easier than to get a child – after a long day at school – to sit in a room set up to look like a classroom and get them to do timed worksheets until they get 100 per cent. Not only that – to do them nightly at home as well, even on Christmas Day. The concept is that if students do the booklets in the right order, they will get a grasp of the subject with barely any teaching involved.

But, as a former Kumon parent myself, I know from personal experience that the reality can be somewhat less sugar-coated. When I tried Kumon with my eldest daughter for about eighteen months, I did spend a lot of money – £60 a month (tellingly, franchisees are told to set the rates according to what the local market will bear) – and we did have a lot of rows. My daughter did also show a very slight improvement in maths, but that instantly disappeared the moment she stopped.

Still, some parents swear by it as a cheaper, more relentless version of traditional tuition – and report much more positive outcomes. And what does it matter if it didn't work for us? Kumon, as we are repeatedly told in the meeting, is 'recession-proof'. When you have young children as your client base, there is, almost literally, one born every minute. To meet that demand, there is also talk in the meeting of moving Kumon sessions out of library back rooms and church halls and into higher-profile sites on the High Street. Here they can have longer opening hours to accommodate the untapped potential of those customers not yet old enough to be at school.

A generation ago in the UK and the US, private tuition was the domain of a small number of middle-class children who were really struggling to keep up or who were trying to prepare for key exams. In the intervening years, that little bit of help has become a must-have. A quarter of school children now get tutoring – up from eighteen per cent five years ago, according to research by the education charity The Sutton Trust.

From traditional one-on-one teaching to group classes and online services, the UK market alone has been estimated at £6 billion per year, and to employ, on and off, one million people. On average, families are estimated to spend £2,758 per year on tutoring. The UK is following in the footsteps of the Far East, where tutoring companies are listed on the stock exchange – and some super-tutors have a cult-like, pop-star following. In Japan, China and Korea, tuition centres are like night schools, tipping pupils into sixteen-hour days, and viewed as an essential part of the education system.

But as Kumon and other companies such as Explore Learning are finding, Western parents are now providing the next big growth market. No longer the preserve of private-school parents, lower-income families are also prepared to pay the money if it means tutors will come to their homes and avoid rows by helping children with their homework. Where once it was a closely kept, even embarrassing, secret that your child got extra help, many families who are new to Britain take exactly the opposite view. Rather they see it as a badge of honour that they are doing all they can to help their children succeed.

As with everything in the education greenhouse, the tutoring system is also overheating. Many perfectly able students now get tuition, not because they need help, but because their parents want to keep them out in front. As Lyndsey, who just got her daughter into a competitive London girls' school, points out: 'It's not just the average or poor students. All that's happened is that the bar has been raised for everyone. No one is prepared to go without the safety blanket.'

Nor are tutors hired to help in just one troublesome subject any more. Well-off families will now employ several different tutors for as many subjects as they can afford – from music theory to French conversation. Elite tutors also report that the über-rich are getting a taste for taking them along for summer-long holidays to make sure their children don't suffer the 'summer slide'.

Tuition starts sooner too. One nursery-school head teacher told me in dismay of coaches hired to prepare two-year-olds for assessment tests for entry into selective private schools. The skills examined include balancing, hopping and colouring-in. 'At that age, tutoring for assessments masks a child's abilities,' she says. 'The child might get into the school. But then a few years down the line, the parents are surprised when the child can't keep up, their confidence is shattered and the school advises them that wasn't the place for their child after all – and could they find somewhere else, please.'

But while some schools covertly endorse tutoring – often as a way to spare themselves the extra work of improving a child's performance

– other head teachers have been vocal about how damaging it can be, albeit without addressing the fact that they helped to create the frantic atmosphere of the industry in the first place.

For one thing, group learning, as with the Kumon model, is so cookie-cutter that it's unlikely to run alongside the curriculum and may teach methods of maths, such as long division, that are completely different from what a child is learning in school, creating confusion. 'The vast majority of heads are not in favour of private tuition,' says Barry Sindall of the Grammar School Heads Association. 'It creates pressure for children and is really about parental anxiety.' Clarissa Farr, High Mistress of St Paul's Girls' School, Hammersmith, has asked parents to come clean about tutoring, describing it as an 'industry which trades on insecurity and exam anxiety, sometimes undermining rather than building confidence'. Sion Humphreys, Policy Adviser at the National Association of Head Teachers, has even gone as far as to call the tutoring industry 'the Wild West of education'.

Furthermore, tutoring can sour relationships at the school gates. Miriam, a mother of three, had tried to hide the fact that her seven-year-old daughter was enrolled at Kumon – only to get busted by another suspicious parent. 'I'd done everything I could to cover my tracks – making sure Grace's Kumon file couldn't be seen on the dashboard of the car – and going a different route from school. Then the other mother came in, walked straight up to me triumphantly and said: "So Grace is having trouble with her maths, then." I could have screamed.' Furthermore, Miriam points out that it quickly turns into a stampede. 'When one mother finds out someone else is doing Kumon, they start doing it too because everyone panics that their child is going to be the one left behind. In one term at our school, six children in the class signed up. Two of the mothers had a stand-up row because one accused the other of distorting the results in the class.'

Despite parting with large sums for tutoring, many parents are not even happy with the results, with some reporting that it made their children's performance *worse*. After all, many children who genuinely need help with a subject already feel stupid, anxious and left behind. Overeager parents often don't realise that private tuition is not the magic bullet it would seem. Put a low-performing pupil one-to-one with a tutor who doesn't know how to handle issues like low academic self-esteem – and a child's confidence can quickly go further downhill.

Yet most tutoring companies require no teaching qualifications of any kind. Some require no more than a GCSE in the subject the tutor is teaching. Unless they are otherwise trained, many tutors can take the old-fashioned approach of shaming or embarrassing a child to get them to perform – or telling them that they do know the answer *really*.

Former head teacher and parent educator Noël Janis-Norton says: 'Tutors are usually experts in their subjects and were usually good students themselves. Therefore they do not have a natural understanding of why a child is getting stuck, or how to simplify a topic or give the child the skill to get unstuck.'

Carolyn Kerr is a former deputy head teacher who tutors in the competitive hotbed of North London. She worries that instead of looking at the whole child, inexperienced tutors also blindly do what the parents say. 'They are likely just to work relentlessly towards exam passes – regardless of what the pupil needs.'

While some tutoring agencies claim to be able to boost predicted results by two clear grades, independent researchers question whether there are any benefits at all. Judy Ireson, Professor of Psychology in Education at the University of London's Institute of Education, led a study which looked at 3,515 children aged 11, 16 and 18. When it was averaged out, tutored pupils scored just less than half a grade higher in their maths GCSEs than pupils who had not been tutored; enough maybe to lift a borderline candidate from a D grade to a C. But in subjects like English, private tutoring was found to have a negligible effect on GCSE results for boys and girls. Ireson said: 'Parents are in a difficult situation, as there's no regulation of tutors and they find them by word of mouth. Sometimes they find good ones and sometimes they don't. That could be having an impact.'

Mother-of-two Elaine hired a student teacher who was a recent Oxbridge graduate to help her eight-year-old son, James, keep up in maths: 'I didn't even check out her qualifications. I just assumed because she had been at Cambridge, she'd be good. But she had no idea of how to deal with children or engage them. Instead she took the approach of sighing loudly and shaking her head in an exasperated fashion if James got the wrong answer. Then she'd leave long, awkward silences, waiting for him to fill the gap with the answer, which only increased his anxiety even more. The result was he not only felt he was doing badly at school. He had that message reinforced at home too.

'Now I would urge parents not to let anyone who is not properly qualified anywhere near their child. It's not only that it's expensive. It steals the time they should spend being children – and it could even make them feel worse about themselves.'

BE CAREFUL WHAT YOU WISH FOR
PART ONE
THE JAPANESE EXPERIENCE

As a group of mothers stood chatting in the playground in Central Tokyo, a little girl disappeared into thin air. Hundreds of police were instantly drafted in to search for two-year-old Haruna Wakayama, but there was no trace of her.

Three days later, one of the mothers who had been in that gaggle of parents that chilly winter's afternoon walked into a police station and confessed to the child's murder. Former nurse Mitsuko Yamada had quietly slipped way, led Haruna to a nearby public toilet and strangled the toddler with her own scarf. Then she had put the body in a rubbish bag, dropped her own two children with her husband and caught the bullet train to her parents' home in the countryside, where she buried Haruna's body in the garden.

If the murder itself was not shocking enough, it was the motive which shook Japan to the core and forced the nation to look again at the competitive education system it had fostered. Three days before the killing, Yamada had received the news that her own daughter of the same age had failed to get one of the twenty sought-after places at the Otowa Kindergarten, a key first step in entry to one of Japan's elite universities. Haruna, the daughter of a neighbour with whom Yamada had a competitive relationship, had been accepted.

Yamada was quoted as saying that she killed the child because she could not live with the constant reminder that her own daughter had been rejected, explaining: 'She hasn't been doing well recently. It hurt me just to look at Haruna.'

However, the murder, 13 years ago, is about far more than a psychotic mother taking competitive parenting to the extreme. Yamada became a symbol of a growing unease inside Japan about what was going wrong in its education system. The admission that 'school envy' motivated the crime threw a searchlight on to the culture of 'entrance exam wars', and prompted a wave of soul-searching about what the pressure was doing to children and parents alike.

Education Minister Hirofumi Nakasone told a news conference: 'If exam-taking from infant age is becoming overheated, we must consider ways to prevent such a situation.' An editorial in the *Tokyo Shimbun* also reported that the conditions that had led to such a terrible crime were not unusual. It read: 'The deranged mental state that led to the murder is created in the daily relationships among housewives living through their children. The challenge…is to penetrate the deeply troubled society of mothers that even produced the motive to kill.'

Indeed, long before the terms 'helicopter parent', 'tiger parent' or 'pushy parent' began to be used in the West, there was the Japanese 'kyoiku mama' – to describe a parent who pours her heart and soul into her offspring's education and bases her worth entirely on her child's success in the public exams on which their lives depend.

Being a kyoiku mama was a full-time job. Mothers took night classes so they could tutor their children at home after school. If children were taken ill, kyoiku mamas were known for sitting at their child's desk for the day to take notes on lessons so their child would not get left behind.

In Japan this is far from the only killing linked to the pressure on parents and children to make the grade. In 2006 Chiaki Onodera strangled her seven-year-old son Sosuke to death with a belt when he refused to go to after-school tuition – attended by more than half of all Japanese schoolchildren – to prepare him for an upcoming entrance exam. Every year it was estimated there were around 400 cases of parents murdering their children and then themselves, usually to escape the humiliation of educational failure.

Yet to the outside world in the early 2000s, Japanese education looked highly successful. As the country's economy started to boom, it was widely admired for the way the system made children get down to the three Rs from the start, and for how it appeared to be producing the most highly trained workforce on the planet.

Everyone wanted to know the secret. Western educators lined up to pour praise on a system which they admired for giving children longer school terms, more homework and Saturday morning lessons. It was jealously noted that two-thirds of children also attended after-school tuition classes.

But as we enter a period of beefing up school standards in a bid to take Japan's place near the top of the global league tables, it's worth first looking at what Japanese children sacrificed to scale those dizzy heights.

In the aftermath of the Second World War, the Japanese education system was restructured along the lines of its Western victors – in particular the American high-school system. But as the country tried to rebuild itself and catch up after its humiliating defeat, the model was pushed to the extremes by the traditions of Japanese workaholism. As part of their duty, parents were exhorted by the Emperor to sacrifice everything for their children in order to rebuild the economy.

Standardised testing became the method by which children were shape-sorted. Success or failure was measured solely on entry to an elite set of universities. The anxiety filtered down to younger and younger children as they had to compete for entry to top nurseries. But it was the words the Japanese used to describe these social changes which perhaps best underline the consequences. The older generation despaired endlessly over what to do about *ockibore* – the generation of under-achieving children who could not keep up with the exacting curriculum. They also referred to *kireru* - the short-fuse generation who, without warning, would go from being docile to violently aggressive.

For their part, students starting using the term *mukatsuku* to describe the irritation they felt with teachers, parents and life. Shockingly for a culture considered so conformist, by 2002 violence in schools had climbed to 29,300 incidents a year, leading to Japanese schoolyards being described as 'battlefields'. The number of 'exam shame' suicides was also alarming. In 2007, Japan ranked first in the G8 countries for female suicides and second for male.

The unforgiving nature of the system meant that Japanese children also scored much lower for happiness and self-esteem than children in other countries. There were unexpected social tangents too. Commentators identified a phenomenon known as 'home avoidance syndrome' in which husbands no longer felt welcome in their own families because of the intense and exclusive relationships between mothers and the children they tutored around the clock. After long days at the office, it was observed that some men preferred to sleep in shelters for the homeless, rather than be viewed as interruptions to home life.

Yet at the same time as Western nations were developing a serious case of education envy, inside Japan the country's own politicians were starting to question where it was all going wrong. Japan's ever-rising results in international test scores stopped being seen as a cause for national pride, and were instead viewed as the inevitable consequence of drilling children 'like trained seals'.

In a desperate attempt to put the brakes on, Japanese education ministers started to relax standards. In 2002, Saturday school was dropped along with more than a third of the curriculum. A new timetable was introduced to try and spark pupils' curiosity and move them away from rote learning. Ministers published white papers on how children needed to have more contact with nature and enjoy more playtime.

Yet tellingly, the watering-down immediately drew condemnation from critics and parents, who instead called for more rigour. When Japan started to slip very slightly down the league tables, there was even more of a backlash against the relaxation of the stringent standards. One educator compared reducing the pressure on children to making the Japanese 'go to war without weapons'.

Rather than welcome the changes – and the improvement to their children's emotional well-being they might bring – parents also panicked that their children were no longer being taught enough at school. To make up for it, they signed up for more tutoring and looked for private schools which still offered six-day-a-week timetables. She had hardly been away, but already the kyoiku mama was back.

Of course there are stark differences between the culture of conformity in Japan and the culture of individuality in the UK. But there are striking similarities too, not least the over-investment of parents in ways to achieve a narrow definition of success. There is also the same political insistence that schools must be more competitive to train a more efficient workforce.

Even with the effort to relieve the pressure, many deep-rooted problems remain, such as *hikikomori* – in which young people take control of their lives by refusing to go to school and withdrawing into their rooms for months or even years. It is estimated to have affected one million young people in Japan at some time in their lives. Most are firstborn sons from middle-class families, who are under the most pressure. Now that the internet means teenagers no longer need to leave their bedrooms to connect with the outside world, researchers are pointing out there are signs the practice is spreading to the West too, in countries such as France, Spain and Italy.

'Parents nowadays are concentrating only on the academic success of their children,' says Hiroshi Kawai, a child psychiatrist for 42 years, who summed up the problem. 'Children live the lives that their parents plan out for them. They don't feel that life is worth living because they don't have anything of their own to live for.'

BE CAREFUL WHAT YOU WISH FOR
PART TWO

CHINA

COMPARE AMY CHUA, THE author of *Battle Hymn of the Tiger Mother*, to Liu Weihua and Zhang Xinwu and she comes out looking like a pussy cat.

Well before Amy was making her daughters practise their instruments four hours a day, Liu and Zhang were credited with turning their daughter Yiting into an overnight celebrity in their native China, the very crucible of tiger parenting. Not for singing or dancing on a TV talent show, which is the way most British children find overnight fame... Instead Yiting became famous for being the paragon of everything a Chinese child should be: she brought honour to her family by winning a full scholarship to Harvard.

The resulting book, *Harvard Girl Liu Yiting: a character training record*, became the must-read manual for other Chinese families also seeking the holy grail of a place at an Ivy League college or Oxbridge. It went on to sell two million copies and spawned seventy copycat versions, including *Yale Girl* and *Ivy League Is Not a Dream*. All were based on the premise that with a strict upbringing and intense hard work any Chinese family could win the dream ticket.

Yiting's parents started early. While still a baby, they deliberately placed toys just out of her reach to make her try harder to get them. At primary school, they timed her work to prepare for exams and encouraged her to hold ice in her hands to improve her endurance.

At the same time as *Harvard Girl* became a best-seller and encouraged young Chinese to join the throng of applicants for the West's most sought-after educational establishments, there was one more development which increased the temperature still further in the global hothouse.

In 2000, the first results of the Programme for International Student Assessment were published, intended to compare education systems around the world. Across the globe, twenty-six countries put forward a representative sample of their fifteen-year-olds to be compared in tests on maths, science and reading.

In the early days, China did not take part. But as the number of participating nations increased, in 2009 it tried its luck. It entered the children of Shanghai, the country's most affluent petri dish of achievement, where eighty per cent of children go on to university.

It was an impressive debut. Immediately Shanghai – which has a population the size of Ghana – entered the chart at number one.

The result triggered an unprecedented wave of panic among Western countries which had already been slipping far behind Far Eastern competitors such as Singapore, Hong Kong, South Korea and Japan. From starting out in the top ten in the first table, the UK had now dropped to twenty-fifth for reading, twenty-eighth for maths and sixteenth for science. American and French pupils also scored poorly.

It was Napoleon who once warned of China: 'Let her sleep, for when she wakes she will shake the world.' When the French emperor gave those words of warning, few could have foreseen the China of the twenty-first century. Now the fact that China appeared – out of nowhere – to be training a vastly more educated workforce, it seemed to confirm that it was not a matter of *if* China would rule the world. It was a question of *when*.

Western politicians rushed to condemn children for not working hard enough. President Obama called on America's youth to 'out-educate' the world. The UK's Education Secretary, Michael Gove, called it a 'Sputnik moment' after the shock the US got when it realised the Soviet Union was pulling ahead in the Space Race, adding: 'We've got to ensure we do better'. He argued that if students in the UK were to match the achievements of their Asian counterparts, 'a higher level of effort is expected on behalf of students, parents and teachers. School days are longer, school holidays are shorter.' The Confederation of British Industry pitched in by saying that the results showed that the UK was 'a long way behind key competitors'.

National pride was also dented. How could the nation that produced Dickens and Shakespeare be so far behind in literacy? 'Britain is the thick man of Europe', screamed one newspaper headline. 'Bottom of the class!' shouted another. The message was loud and clear. We'd better crack down on education or else we'd be done for. But when it comes to children, you have to be careful what you wish for – let alone how you want to achieve it.

Contrasting Western and Eastern education has never been a comparison of like with like. A closer look at the classrooms which produce these results shows that like Japan, China's success comes at a high cost. And it's the Chinese themselves who are the first to admit it.

On the face of it, the first thing you would notice if you were to walk into an average Shanghai secondary is that the classes are larger, with around forty pupils – roughly double the size of Britain.

There are no discipline problems. Pupils stand to attention to address teachers. To help their voices reach the back, instructors are fitted with microphone headsets. The pace of the average maths lesson is fast and intense, based on a steady rhythm of teachers calling out questions and pupils replying en masse.

In China children spend more than a month longer in school per year than their Western counterparts, and the school day lasts nine hours – with breaks for eye massages to reduce eye strain and physical activity to keep concentration levels high.

The school bell is just the end of the first shift. Children then move on to cram schools. These are taken so seriously that in neighbouring South Korea – and across the Far East – inspectors launch lightning raids to enforce curfews to prevent them teaching pupils past 10 p.m.. At one point the Korean government tried to ban them. But even the law could not suppress a culture in which children live by the following motto: 'Sleep five hours a night and fail. Sleep four hours a night and pass.'

Children also pay a physical price for their dedication to schoolwork. One study found that up to ninety per cent of Asian schoolchildren – including those living in China, Taiwan, Japan, Singapore and South Korea – are nearsighted. This was put down to them spending too much time indoors studying and not enough time outside in the sunlight. By comparison, the overall rate of myopia in the UK is between twenty and thirty per cent.

Nor are children thriving under the pressure. A third of Chinese primary-school children display symptoms of stress as a result of China's fiercely competitive education system and pushy parenting, according to one recent study. Youngsters as young as six are affected, according to British and Chinese researchers led by Professor Therese Hesketh at University College London. The survey of nine- to twelve-year-olds in the eastern province of Zhejiang found that more than eighty per cent worried 'a lot' about exams, while two-thirds feared punishment by their teachers. Almost three-quarters were scared of physical punishment by their parents.

Crucially, the price the students in Shanghai pay for their success is also high. A 2009 study found that twenty-four per cent of 2,500 students there had thought about killing themselves, mostly in response to exam pressure. As in Japan, it's also the words that the Chinese use that give a real insight into what is happening within. Now in common usage is the term *gaofen dineng*, meaning students who get high scores but have low ability. Such young people are said to spend so much time studying that they never learn to take initiative or become creative. After Shanghai again ranked first for mathematics, science and reading in 2013, the leader of the Shanghai PISA programme Zhang Minxuan urged parents not to overburden children with homework and to cut back on tutoring so they 'can have more time for individual development'.

Yet despite the clear evidence that oriental children work harder, it is not just what goes on within the classroom that marks the difference between Far Eastern and Western children. It is also what is going on within the home.

From an early age, Chinese children are raised to believe that education is the only way; not just by their parents, but by their entire families. That includes grandparents, uncles and aunts who won't shrink from reminding youngsters that an A is required in every test to bring honour to the family. While our children are brought up being told 'be yourself', Chinese youngsters are raised with the saying 'study hard or you'll grow up a beggar' ringing in their ears. The Confucian tradition of unfailing filial obedience means that a Chinese child is more likely to listen, too.

Tellingly, another hot-selling parenting book found on the shelves next to *Harvard Girl* is called *That's Why They Go to Peking University*. In this companion work, eagle dad Xiao Baiyou expounds his philosophy of 'teaching with sticks' and tells of how beating his three children helped them land places at the wowrld's top colleges.

The Chinese approach to education is rooted in traditions that have grown up over thousands of years. In other words, it would take more than adding a few extra hours to the school day and more testing to make British children work like this. It would take a complete cultural personality transplant. However much politicians want British children to rise up the league tables, it certainly won't happen by the time the next three-yearly PISA test comes round again.

But of course the supreme irony of all this is the fact that despite being the envy of every country, like the Japanese the Chinese are also calling their education system a failure. At the same time as Western governments strive to make their schools more Asian, Asian governments are trying to make their schools more European and creative.

While we fret here about poor maths scores, the Chinese point to another test, which did not grab the headlines, which found that in tests of creativity and imagination, Chinese children came fifth from bottom. 'The results are shocking,' the *China Daily* warned. 'Children had almost no chance to use their imagination. From the first day of school they are pushed into a culture of exams, exams and more exams.'

Other educators have also stepped forward to point out that unless Far Eastern economies stop imitating and start innovating, they will never live up to their promise. Despite producing some of the most highly educated people in the world, the McKinsey & Company consulting firm has warned of 'China's Looming Talent Shortage'. As a result, Chinese universities are changing their admissions policies to encourage more imaginative applicants. Changes under discussion at the Chinese Ministry of Education include stopping written homework for primary school pupils and encouraging parents to enrol kids in extra-curricular activities to produce more well-rounded children. More and more Chinese parents are also seeking to educate their children at home, because so much corporal punishment is meted out in schools. There has even been a boom in alternative education such as Waldorf (Steiner) schools in China. In one recent survey, four out of ten Chinese parents said they wanted to send their children to the more liberal West to study.

Peking University High School deputy principal and teacher Jiang Xueqin is damning in his assessment of the Chinese education style. 'It's a test-oriented education system, which means that students are taught from a very early age how to beat tests. The failings of a rote-memorisation system are well known: lack of social and practical skills, absence of self-discipline and imagination, loss of curiosity and passion for learning. 'One way we'll know we're succeeding in changing China's schools is when those scores come down.'

ANOTHER WAY?

O N THE DAY I gave birth to my first child in 2001, I never considered I was also providing another footsoldier in the battle to keep Britain economically ahead.

When I was growing up, the UK was still a world power, a big player; the home of Dickens, Shakespeare and one of the most widely used languages on Earth. If I'm honest, I assumed that I did not need to worry about my daughter's role in the economy of the future. Smugly perhaps, I assumed she had all the head start she needed.

Then, as we have seen, global league tables baldly demonstrated that nations which had previously posed no threat to us in the world order were producing children who, on paper at least, far outperformed ours. Longer school days, shorter holidays, more tests and homework – all done with more 'rigour' – are all being touted as the only solution. But as the experience of the Japanese, Chinese and Korean education systems shows us, politicians and parents have to be careful what they wish for.

Let's not forget, though, that there is another nation which regularly excels in the PISA chart, and which works very differently from the Far Eastern model. It topped the PISA league tables in the first year and has more-or-less stayed in the top five best-performing countries ever since – the only European nation to do so. As Asian countries became increasingly competitive for the top spots, it was only in 2013 that Finland slipped out of the top ten for Maths out of 65 nations.

Finland is a country where actual schooling does not start until seven, by which time children are thirsty for knowledge, and where they get virtually no homework. Pupils have no formal tests until the age of 16. There are no school inspectors or internal rankings. Instead of public exams, the progress of pupils is monitored in the classroom by highly qualified teachers. There is no competition to get into schools either, because all are considered equally good.

All this sounds like a miracle. But the reforms have taken more than forty years to implement. The changes started in the late 1960s when the Finns got rid of two-tier private and public education. In the 1980s they scrapped streaming. In the 1990s they abolished schools inspectors. It's also a culture which puts a high value on the independence and individuality of pupils. Children walk or bicycle to school by themselves – and work cooperatively in mixed sets in the classroom.

Finnish kids also top the chart for one other essential measure. The country also has some of the world's happiest children. It scores fourth for childhood well-being, according to UNICEF. The UK comes sixteenth, and the US twenty-sixth. It may also be no coincidence that Finland scores highly in rankings of 'study effectiveness'. Crucially, pupils spend fewer hours in the classroom – around seven hours per day compared with sixteen hours in China – but still get some of the best results.

Of course, not all these lessons are directly transferable. Finland is a smaller country and it has less of a problem with child poverty. Yet the performance of Finland's children demonstrates there are ways of helping youngsters do well – without making them miserable.

DOES COMPETITION MAKE CHILDREN DO BETTER?

W E LIVE IN A culture in which we are told that not only is competition a fact of life – it's actually good for us.

From the moment our children are born, parents preach the message that they have to compete to be number one. From who is the cutest little girl to the best little kicker on the toddler soccer team, we educate our offspring that life has to be a continual contest. In today's world, what other choice do we have? Phrases like 'law of the jungle', 'every man for himself' and 'dog eat dog' underline our belief that we have to win, whatever happens.

Even when we see our children getting upset and anxious, it still feels like it's the only way. We tell ourselves that kids had better get used to it because that's the way life is. Aren't we just being good parents by toughening them up to get them ready for the big, bad world? Of course we insist that we are encouraging them when we say 'Do your best'. But in today's competitive atmosphere, aren't we really telling them to *be* the best?

Educator Alfie Kohn has been studying, writing and speaking on the effects of competition for nearly thirty years. In his review of the evidence spanning several decades, he says studies show time and time again that competition does not make our children perform better. By definition, most people lose in competitive encounters. But the winners don't necessarily find it any easier either. As soon as the moment of victory passes, they become nervous about how they are going to stay on top.

Try applying what this means to schools. As testing starts earlier and earlier, it means kids who don't do well right away can tend to write themselves off early on. Those who do get off to a good start find they have to continually compete to maintain their feelings of self-worth.

Kohn says: 'Success comes to be defined as victory, even though these are really two very different things. Even when the child manages to win, the whole affair, psychologically speaking, becomes a vicious circle: the more he competes, the more he needs to compete to feel good about himself.'

Our children have not had time to work out their own strengths, before they get judged in contests they didn't ask to compete in. When parents pile on the pressure at home at the same time as schools are upping the ante, children can feel judged on their performance whichever way they turn.

The irony is that all this competition doesn't make our children fly higher. In studies spanning nearly sixty years, sixty-five found that children learn better when they work cooperatively as opposed to competitively, eight found the reverse – and thirty-six found no big difference.

The more difficult and complex the task, the worse participants perform, because anxiety stands in the way of allowing them to think through the problem. In test situations, brain power that would be better spent working out the answer is spent worrying about how good competitors' answers are. Brain scans of people trying to solve puzzles have found that the fear centres are more likely to be activated when players are told they are competing. This diversion of their brain power means that it takes them longer to find the answer. In short, competition increases stress and sends the brain into fight-or-flight mode. That then short-circuits its ability to work. While we might compete better in encounters we feel likely to win, it's another story if we feel like the underdog.

So instead of allowing kids to develop a secure base from which to develop safely, making children compete from an early age takes away the very foundation from which they can grow strong and secure. While there is nothing wrong with success, the question we should ask is whether we should teach children that their success must always be at the expense of other people's. In order to win, does everyone else have to fail? By teaching children it's every man for himself out there, we are making the world feel like a very lonely place to be.

But is there any alternative? After all, isn't competition, as they say, an instinct? Even though Charles Darwin never actually coined the phrase, we constantly talk of 'survival of the fittest' as if it were the driving force of our society. However, anthropologists studying animal behaviour aren't sure it's so cut and dried. While there is certainly competition for mates and resources if they are scarce, there are also plenty of examples of cooperation to be found in the animal kingdom when things are more plentiful.

While chimpanzees compete with each other and fight aggressively for limited food and mates, their close cousins, the bonobos – which live in more bountiful climes – care for each other's children, have open sexual relationships and work together to find food.

Civilisation itself is testament to the fact that we cooperate, more than we compete. The theory that competition is our prime driving force is also contradicted by the fact that some cultures, such as in the US for example, are much more competitive than others. Yet as parents we perform twists and turns to make our children conform to the cultural norms. In America, parents constantly insist that competition is essential for kids' confidence. In more cooperative societies such as Mexico, researchers have found that parents take another view. They assert that their children get confidence from working with others.

The race between the US and Russia to get the first man on the Moon is often used as an example of how competition can be used to drive us forward. But as Kohn points out, think how much sooner the human race would have got there if the two superpowers had shared their expertise. Indeed, studies have found that when children are encouraged to work together they are not only happier to share their talents and feel good about themselves; they are also more creative.

In one study, children were asked to make 'silly collages'. Some competed for prizes and some didn't. Seven artists then rated the kids' work. The result was that the kids who were trying to win made pictures that were less creative. The children who were not under the same pressure let their brains run free.

BENDING THE RULES

WHY CHEATING IS ON THE RISE

H ERE ARE A FEW quick statistics.

The number of students caught cheating at top universities has surged since 2011. OxbridgeEssays.com – an essay-writing company – says it gets more than 10,000 orders a year from school pupils and university students. Nine out of ten children feel under pressure to win when they play sport. Two-thirds say that this has led them to cheat, with top tactics including faking injury and time-wasting. As many as one in ten UK students and one in six US students admit to using cognitive performance-enhancing drugs such as Ritalin to stay alert and improve academic results – to the extent that some institutions are thinking about introducing drug testing.

Nor is it just a problem in the West. In China, female students have been banned from wearing bras and all candidates are asked to go through metal detectors to seek out wireless listening devices before they take the university entrance exams, known as *gaokao*. Websites such as SpyStudent.com openly sell wrist and pen cameras that send images to helpers outside the exam halls who then send back the messages via devices inserted into students' ears.

Of course, cheating is as old as school inkwells. But there is still plenty of evidence to show that it is on the rise. Nor is the increase just down to the fact that it's easier these days to smuggle technology into the exam hall – or cut and paste an essay off the internet.

Eric Anderman, Professor of Educational Psychology at Ohio State University, has been studying cheating in schools for decades. His research has found that it goes up when students believe that the point of learning is only to get exam results, and when they are constantly compared.

However, it's not just the pupils who are bending the rules. In today's educational pressure cooker, teachers, heads and parents also feel they have no choice but to play the system. More teachers are being censured for giving inappropriate assistance to candidates, according to exam watchdogs in the UK. In 2013, they revealed that 135 schools were issued with penalties for giving candidates extra time, inappropriate invigilation or bungling the handling of test papers in exams over the summer. Staff were also rapped for giving candidates the answer in the exam rooms or allowing them extra time to finish papers.

Tiger parents are also increasingly being caught out. The number who lodged claims that their children were ill with ailments such as hay fever and headaches during their A levels and GCSE exams (in order to get marks added) has gone up by a suspiciously large amount in the last five years – no less than twenty per cent.

Lies and misrepresentation are now just seen as what you have to do to get the best for your child. The number of council investigations into parents fraudulently trying to get their children into schools by using false addresses or lying about their religion has rocketed eleven-fold over the same period.

Head teachers are not immune either. In independent schools, league tables are manicured by only allowing children they know will get excellent passes to take certain subjects, and suggesting that weaker candidates go elsewhere before crunch A level and GCSE tests. In comprehensives, heads have been found sending troublesome pupils home during inspections without officially recording the absences, so their schools get rated more highly.

This is a problem that social scientists and psychologists say is unlikely to go away. Stanford psychology professor Carol Dweck believes that cheating is more likely to happen when schools stop being seen as places to learn and develop, but merely as theatres in which to demonstrate pupils' intelligence by means of grades. As the importance of doing well continues to increase, the temptation to cheat only becomes more inviting.

At the same time, the number of parents taking their children out of the education system is soaring. In the UK alone, local councils have seen the number of children being taught at home rise by more than sixty per cent. According to a recent House of Commons schools select committee, up to 150,000 children are taught outside mainstream schools, and the number is 'believed to be growing steadily' – due mainly to the amount of testing in schools.

Indeed, it's a global trend. In the US, where a standardised curriculum is also bearing down on schools, the number of home-schooled pupils has risen by thirty-six per cent over five years.

Many parents say they are opting out because it's the best way to ensure that their child is treated like an individual, and there is growing evidence that these children do not suffer. Far from disappearing into oblivion, they perform better. There are signs too that universities in the US and the UK are starting to prefer pupils educated outside of mainstream schooling because they think more independently and creatively.

While home-schooling is only a solution for a small number of families, it is proof perhaps that it is possible to step off the merry-go-round of competitive parenting – and still help your child reach their potential.

PART TWO

HOW COMPETITIVE PARENTING AND SCHOOLING AFFECT OUR CHILDREN

Bella was six when she first started saying she hated doing sums. Her parents came to dread the nights when she brought home her maths homework, because their daughter would barely get her books out of her bag before yelling 'I'm stuck!'

When they tried to sit down and help her, their child was reluctant to try any part of the work herself. One wrong word – even a gentle reminder about how to approach the question or a suggestion that she could work out the answer after all – would prompt a hysterical reaction. If Bella did say something, it was usually a wild guess. Her behaviour – including slithering off her chair like a snake – looked like she was doing anything to avoid engaging her brain. Most sessions would end with Bella putting her head in her hands and shouting 'I'm stupid, aren't I?' and throwing her books on the floor.

At parents' evening, Bella's teacher seemed to take the view that she was simply not academically very able. It did not help that the teacher had already made no secret of the fact that Bella was not sitting on the table expected to do well in the SATs tests.

Worried that she had a learning difficulty such as dyscalculia – the numerical equivalent of dyslexia – Bella's parents Sophie and Simon took her to an educational psychologist. She found that Bella was of above average cognitive ability and had no obvious issues. What the educational psychologist did identify, though, was Bella's innate lack of confidence. She just didn't *believe* she could do maths.

Early on at school, maths had become coded in Bella's mind as 'dangerous', making her flight-or-fight reflex kick in. In other words, her brain would simply switch off when things got challenging. At exactly the moment when she needed her intellect to work at its best, her access to her working memory was cut off. Quite literally, her mind went blank.

At school, during her frequent quick-fire mental maths tests, Bella seemed calm enough, but spent most of the time looking around the room and fretting that her classmates were getting the answers right while she was getting them wrong. Like many children with academic anxieties, she saved the hysteria for when she was at home.

It had never been Sophie's intention to pressure her daughter. As a high-flying professional who had done well at a high-achieving school herself, she just naturally expected her child to follow in her footsteps. It never occurred to her that she was a tough act to follow.

Often stressed herself due to work pressures, including demanding bosses who emailed and rang her around the clock, Sophie found it hard to stay calm when Bella showed so much distress. Sometimes, when she felt she could not get through to her child, she lost her temper, telling her to 'pull herself together'. As she watched Bella sinking to the bottom of the class, Sophie only became more anxious around her daughter.

All she wanted to do was give her some suggestions about how to do better – but somehow they didn't come out that like. It was not that she wanted to be pushy, although it may have looked like that to the outside world; she just couldn't bear to see her child's confidence sink ever lower.

But all Bella heard when her mother tried to help was carping criticism. Bella gave herself a hard enough time about her lack of success – without her mother telling her to try harder. In order to limit the target that her mother could aim for, Bella closed down, becoming secretive about her tests and uncommunicative about school. When her mother walked into her bedroom to talk about her day, Bella would find an excuse to walk out.

When Bella had gone to bed, Sophie would complain to her

husband about how sulky and difficult she was. What was wrong with that child? Hadn't they given her everything? What had they done to deserve such an ungrateful daughter? Simon took the view that Bella was lazy and just needed to get on with it.

By this time, Sophie was also working harder to pay for a £60-an-hour tutor, something she secretly resented because Bella still refused to apply herself, making it feel like money down the drain.

It was one afternoon when Sophie went to collect her daughter from school – and realised that she was dreading, not looking forward to, seeing the child she once couldn't bear to be apart from – that she decided she had to get help.

The next day she rang a parenting counsellor to see if she could diagnose what was wrong with Bella. But after listening to a summary of the issues, the therapist told her it was not Bella she needed to see. It was Sophie and Simon. After a session in which she heard the couple explain the deterioration of their relationship with their daughter, they were stopped in their tracks by being told: 'It sounds as if Bella feels very criticised. I think you are in danger of losing your connection with your child.'

BELLA'S STORY IS NOT EXTREME, BUT TYPICAL

I HAVE CHOSEN BELLA as an example of the effect the competitive world can have on our children, but not because she is the most extreme example. Far from it. One in ten children aged five to sixteen in the UK has a clinically diagnosable mental health problem, much worse than Bella's. But while not all those cases will be linked to stress at school by any means, it certainly won't have helped.

In fact I chose Bella because she is one of the more representative examples. Bella's story is typical of how even children in the most secure, affluent and loving homes can suffer in this pressure-cooker atmosphere. Bella's fears about her performance could not be solved by simply telling her to 'try harder'. Longer school days, more testing or higher standards would not have made her 'do better'.

If her parents had not sought help, abruptly changed direction and taken the pressure off, Bella would have only grown more alienated from both her family – and her schooling. Furthermore, studies show that her biting self-criticism and negative view of the world at such a young age would have also made her much more at risk of developing anxiety disorders and depression as she got older. Half of people with lifelong mental health problems experience their first symptoms by the age of fourteen.

As a sensitive child, Bella's fears about her abilities and the disappointment they triggered in the adults around her cut to the very core of her feelings of self-worth. To the outside world, Sophie could have been classified a typical tiger mother. In her panic, she tried everything from tutoring to enriching extra-curricular activities to stop her child from sinking into the quicksand. The truth was that both mother and child were caught in a Catch-22 situation, where Bella felt she could do nothing right – so it was not worth even trying.

Of course, how children react to pressure will depend on the temperaments of everyone involved, and the relationship between children and parents. Psychologists have observed that some securely attached children may feel safe enough to risk acting up to show their distress. A less securely bonded child may drive their feelings of anxiety underground – or find other ways to secure approval. By buying into and reinforcing the competitive culture of schooling, instead of acting as a bumper against them, loving parents like Sophie and Simon unwittingly became part of their daughter's problem.

It's easy to mock pushy parents. In our culture, they are portrayed as sharp-elbowed harridans who demand feedback on why their child didn't get the starring part in the school play – and want photo finishes on sports days. It's also fun to laugh at the shenanigans of the section of society that is supposed to be made up of the responsible, sensible ones.

Even competitive parents make fun of other competitive parents in an effort to distance themselves. But though it may feel comfortable to demonise these parents, the truth is that most feel they have no choice but to be 'pushy'. Almost every mum and dad who gets involved in their child's education feels obliged to work behind the scenes to make sure they do well – or at least that they are able to keep their head above water.

Studies show that involved parenting *does* improve your child's chances of success. But taken to extremes or done without great care and sensitivity, the law of diminishing returns kicks in. Taken beyond that point, as we shall see, pushing too hard can do serious damage to both your child and your relationship with them.

HOW THE THREAT TO OUR CHILDREN HAS CHANGED

As I said in my introduction, it looks, on the surface, as if our children have never had it so good.

Today the bedroom of the average child looks like an Aladdin's cave of treasures. When totted up, the average teenager owns £5,257 worth of gadgets, £1,000 worth of clothes and £250 worth of trainers, according to one survey. Outside our front doors, our children are probably safer from disease, war and violence than at any other time in human history.

Instead, the threat has moved inside – into our homes and schools, where the same privileged children are subject to more prodding and pressure than ever before. All the fun whiteboards and educational learning games that are now features of modern classrooms don't make up for the fact that our children know they are under pressure to perform at every level.

And, while advances in nutrition and healthcare mean that a child born today can expect to live until the age of 100, the conditions in which we are raising our children mean they are also the unhappiest generation in history. YoungMinds, the children's mental health charity, estimates that nearly one million children between the ages of five and fifteen now have mental health problems such as depression or anxiety, and the numbers look set to keep on rising.

ChildLine, the kids' advice service, also says there is a steady rise in the number of calls it receives about exam stress. They report that young people talk about being 'panic-stricken, overburdened and overwhelmed', because it feels as if their whole future depends on the results.

If not addressed by adolescence, children don't only suffer feelings of nervousness and inadequacy. They are also more likely to develop more severe conditions such as self-harming and eating disorders, and they may also seek escape through drugs, drink and meaningless sex.

At the same time that children are facing tougher standards, they are also the most distracted generation in history. With most schools now setting homework to be done on the computer, with the best will in the world, it's hard to ignore the endless notifications alerting you to the fact that someone, somewhere on social networks is talking about you. For girls, more often than not, it means being rated on your looks and body. So-called brainy girls could once be bluestockings. Now they have to be babes as well.

While we parents may have vied to see who had the coolest school bag when we are were at school, nowadays young people are judging each other in countless other arenas: their phones, laptops, clothes, popularity and sex appeal.

While previous generations of children could go home after school and close their bedroom door behind them, these days there is no escape from the internet – and the cyber-bullying and social competition that it brings.

At the same time as piling on the pressure, we are also taking away our children's ability to cope – by allowing them less downtime, less time to play, less interaction with nature and less time and opportunity to get to know themselves. Before they know who they are, they have adults and peers telling them who they ought to be.

Of course, there has always been competition in childhood. O levels and A levels have long been milestones in our education system which set the course of our futures. But what is different today is how early testing starts – and how relentless it is. Where once children were examined when they were old enough for their intellectual capacities to develop, early years curricula mean they are now assessed when they are barely out of nappies. At primary schools, pupils once sat low-key exams set in school by their teachers. Now children are regularly put through public tests and told that the reputation of their teachers and schools rides on the results.

Equally, the first year of the sixth form used to be a time when pupils could get deeply engrossed in three, or at the most four, specialised subjects. Now no sooner have they emerged from the pressure of trying to rack up as many As and A*s in their GCSEs as possible than they are plunged into one-year AS level courses, based on which their university places are decided.

Even with asterisks sprinkled like glitter all over their results, their whole futures might still have to be decided by a 5,000-word dissertation on a completely different subject for the Extended Project Qualification, which serves as a tie-breaker between university applicants.

A generation ago, it was good enough to excel in one or two areas. Now average is no longer good enough – to be considered truly successful, a child is expected to do well across the board. If they are not an all-rounder, a child will be chivvied and coached and told to squeeze in more extra-curricular activities until they at least give a passing impression of being one.

Just to demoralise them even more, children are being told that they have to work harder to get the same grades because apparently until now it's all been too easy – and children in completely different cultures in the Far East get better results than them. The world that once seemed to be their oyster has now – apparently – dramatically snapped shut. No longer do decent grades promise a place at a good university.

And even once they have their degree, while previous generations left university more or less debt-free and secure in the knowledge that they would find jobs to match their qualifications, today's young people today graduate with no guarantees and owing perhaps tens of thousands in tuition fees. For the first time in history, graduates are routinely working for free – and in some cases even paying to work for companies. No wonder our children feel so hopeless.

THE RISE OF STRESS IN CHILDREN

In a dimly-lit room, painted with soothing underwater scenes, primary school pupils sit in crocodile formation on the floor, massaging one another. The children stay in uniform – but their small hands work carefully on the back, head, arms and shoulders of the classmate in front of them.

A few years ago, New Brighton Primary School in Wallasey, Merseyside used a government grant to create a dedicated Quiet Place, complete with a mini waterfall, a relaxation chair and aromatherapy oils. To decompress, pupils also get to use computer software which attaches sensors to their fingertips and flashes up calming images of meadows, flowers and babbling brooks.

Not so long ago the idea that a child could be 'stressed' would have seemed laughable. Spa treatments like this would have been a rare treat for only the most highly strung of adults. Now New Brighton is one of sixty primaries around the country where pupils are taught massage as a relaxation technique. Just as stress has become one of the biggest problems for adults in the British workplace – the cost to the economy is estimated at £3.7 billion a year – it is also filtering down to children.

Of course stress is nothing new. It's an essential survival mechanism which enables us to enter flight-or-fight mode and escape from dangerous situations, such as being pursued by a predator. But biologically, our brains are wired to deal only with short injections of stress hormones into the bloodstream. In modern life, though, it can feel like the drip-feed of stress is almost constant.

Physiologically, there is no difference in the way adults and children process stress, hence the rise in adult patterns of stress-related behaviour in children as young as three. After all, hothoused toddlers are never left to just 'be', children are never left to just play, teenagers are never left just to think – because we don't trust them with their iPhones or iPads.

Now there is not only the rush hour for work. There's also the race to nursery and childminder as bewildered toddlers are pushed at breakneck speed by parents desperate to get to the office – and get back in time to escape late fees.

Unlike adults, children have no control over their lives. They also lack the understanding, vocabulary and resources to deal with the constant anxiety that they live with. By the time they are in the throes of their careers, grown-ups have learnt how chatting to a friend might help, how a visit to the gym might let off some steam and how an early night can make tomorrow feel like a better day. Children have neither the knowledge nor experience to recognise how they feel or know how to cope.

Even though schools now place the same sort of high-performance demands and performance reviews on children as workplaces do on us, we make no allowances. According to one survey, one in three primary school children in Birmingham were so stressed by SATs tests that they couldn't eat or sleep. Almost half – forty-eight per cent – of children couldn't concentrate because they were so worried. Forty-three per cent admitted that they were worried they would let their families down.

The Priory, the clinic made famous by its celebrity patients suffering from addiction and depression, now has specialist centres for adolescents.

And just as stress has become the number-one cause of long-term workplace absence, so children are refusing to go to school. One in five British children have suffered from a 'phobia' of going to school.

Our goal cannot realistically be to have children who never suffer any stress. But we can aim for the right amount for their personality type and personal threshold.

Studies have found that 'butterflies' in your stomach can enhance performance. But if there are too many stress hormones, your performance drops off and you lose the ability to memorise and process information. Children experience 'good' stress when they feel in control and confident that they can perform well in a challenge – and when the pressure is short-term. They experience 'bad' stress when they feel helpless and as if their anxiety is never going to end.

Because children may be unable to find the words to express what they are feeling, they are also more likely to internalise their emotions than adults – which can then show in the form of psychosomatic symptoms such as unexplained stomach pains and headaches. Yet for a parent it can be extremely difficult to spot the warning signs and tell them apart from normal childhood behaviour or ailments.

One of Bella's classmates, ten-year-old Jasmine, dealt with her worries in a different way. Rather than avoid her homework, she would stay up late into the night to repeatedly re-do it so it was perfect for the morning. One crossing-out was enough to make her rip up her work and start again.

Naturally, her teachers praised Jasmine to the hilt for her beautifully presented compositions. Once thrilled that their daughter seemed to be so conscientious, by Year Six Jasmine's parents became so worried about her perfectionist streak they started bribing her to go to bed.

In the mornings, Jasmine would also make and re-make her bed three or four times, smoothing out every wrinkle and carefully placing every soft toy in the same order around the edge. If anyone tried to sit on the bed – even her cat – she became upset and angry. Yet she struggled to explain why it was so important to her.

This ritual had knock-on effects. The time it took to perform meant that Jasmine then became anxious about being late for school. Still, she couldn't seem to tear herself away until she had done it to her satisfaction.

Also in the class was Jack, who developed a general anxiety disorder after dropping to the bottom set. He got extra help at school as well as tutoring. But Jack felt stigmatised by the fact that his classmates knew he needed support. There were lots of surprise tests in Year Six, so the teacher often asked the pupils to mark each other's work. Jack's humiliation was compounded when other children saw his bad marks. As his self-image was still forming, he believed that was the way it would always be.

Bella and Jasmine's anxieties were hidden at school, while Jack's were more visible. When he felt his panic rising, he tried to avoid stressful situations by frequently disappearing to the toilet. The problem was that the longer he spent there, the more worried he was about coming back in case the other children wondered what he had been doing. Indeed, the other kids started calling him 'weird'.

If not addressed at primary school, anxiety issues such as these tend to become even more pronounced – and potentially more serious – at secondary.

Andrea was in Year Nine. Andrea lost her confidence somewhere along the way at primary school and it had never recovered. As she headed towards GCSEs, her life was punctuated by frequent rows with her desperately worried mother, Sally. Sally had long ago given up wanting her daughter to get top marks. All she wanted was for Andrea to take responsibility for her studies and do some work before it was too late.

But Andrea had taken the route of dealing with her low academic self-esteem by avoiding work altogether. She wrote the minimum in her homework diary, forgetting to note down test dates and what she needed to revise. Her negative view of her abilities was then confirmed when she got poor results.

She attended an acclaimed academy which was supposed to excel at bringing out the best in all its pupils. But until that point, rather than anyone addressing the root cause of her behaviour, Andrea's exercise books had been covered in angry red ink and threats from her teachers. Andrea had been offered the chance to attend self-esteem workshops, but somehow always seemed to miss them, a fact which had yet to be noticed or followed up by the pastoral staff.

Andrea started refusing to go to school. The procrastination and late nights spent struggling with her mother over her homework (Andrea found it easier to row with her mother than get down to it) – meant that she sometimes did not get to bed until 11pm. Because she had to be up at 6.45am, she was even more tired and emotional in the mornings.

As Andrea's dad had already left for work by then, Sally had no help to haul her physically bigger daughter out of bed. At a loss for what to do, Sally took to doing deals with her daughter to make her promise to go to school in the future – if she just phoned in sick for her. Just this once.

Also in Andrea's year was Laura. She was the sort of wholesome, pretty girl you would expect to see beaming from the pages of the *Daily Telegraph* in August to illustrate record numbers of students getting straight As and A*s.

An all-rounder who also played hockey for her school, Laura openly declared that she expected herself to stay in the top set for everything. However, her careers adviser had recently advised that as well as her demanding sports schedule, she would do well to take up more extra-curricular activities to beef up her applications for elite universities.

REAL-LIFE EXPERIENCES

'Among girls, it's peer pressure as well. There is a girl in my fourteen-year-old daughter's year group who annoyed the rest of the class because she said she always had to come top in every subject. So the other girls got together and each gave each other one subject each to come first in to knock her off the perch.'

Caroline, mother of three

'I don't feel like I go to school to be educated. I feel like I go to get good marks, to get me into university and then into a high-flying job – and that is supposed to lead to happiness. It's very important to me that I come first. I compare my marks and when my score is lower, I try and work harder.'

Tara, 15

'I feel in order to get into a top university I can't afford to have a life. But there seems no option. If you don't do everything, you won't make it – and if you don't get into an elite university then you are a loser. We're so stuck.'

Edward, 17

'On a good day, I don't get much more than about six hours of sleep because I have so much homework. On a bad day, I might stay up to two in the morning. Some of my other friends in the sixth form have stayed up all night. We have to rely on catching up on sleep on the weekends.'

Madeleine, 17

Laura's parents no longer needed to push her – she had her own ultra-high academic standards to live up to. Her mother would have loved nothing better than for her daughter to relax more, especially as Laura had started refusing to take a break even during the school holidays. When her mum suggested a week-long sunshine get-away at Easter, Laura refused to go, saying that she would not be able to take all her books – and it would be easier to revise for her mocks in her bedroom than on a beach.

Laura's anxiety came to the surface when she started suffering panic attacks before exams. She also became hysterical when she got eighty-two per cent on one science test, telling her mother – who was perfectly pleased with the result – that she should have done better.

Such a drive for perfectionism can run very high in girls, who are more malleable in their early years and want to be 'good', and are more likely than boys to rate their worth by their last test score. Now that girls are outperforming boys and have similar opportunities in the workplace, such a drive is made more acute by the fact that many loving parents tend to set the highest goals for their daughters.

Even if the parents do not express it, the unspoken sense their children should do well can still pervade the atmosphere of a home. Without realising it, parents create a feeling that everyone must excel, particularly if they set a lot of store by maintaining an image of being a 'successful' family.

While some girls will rise to the challenge, others will cave in under the pressure. On top of that, as they reach their teenage years, girls are also beset by the burden of trying to conform to very narrow ideals of physical beauty. It's not just vanity. Today's girls know they also risk being ostracised by their contemporaries if they fall short.

According to Professor Carrie Paechter of Goldsmiths College, University of London, girls feel a particular pressure to perform brilliantly in everything – from sport to academic subjects. 'There are girls in private schools who are "projects" of their parents, learning two or three instruments to grade eight standard and excelling in sport and academia because they feel that is what is expected of them… But a few of them end up in anorexia clinics complaining that their schools only cared about their results.

'Good schools need to start looking at girls and saying "This is too much, you do too many things." Good schools need to start saying "You can't do that many A levels, even if you want to."'

Another demonstration of the pressure to succeed is the rising number of reports of self-harm. Sue Minto, head of ChildLine, says the issue is now in the top five main worries for fourteen-year-old children – and it's starting younger than ever.

The 2012 statistics from the NHS found that hospitals treated more than 18,000 girls and 4,600 boys age between ten and nineteen who had deliberately self-harmed – a rise of eleven per cent compared with the previous year. Numbers have also risen by thirty per cent for youngsters aged between ten and fourteen. ChildLine said it had carried out 47,000 counselling sessions in the previous twelve months for children who self-harmed, a forty per cent rise on the previous year.

Self-harm has long been with us – in different ways. Most of us knew someone at school who bit their nails until they bled or chewed their hair. But now parents and schools are facing self-harming in more serious forms – and it appears to be extremely contagious, thanks in part to dedicated websites and some young adult books which have chosen it as a 'sexy', provocative new theme. The result is that it can spread through classes like wildfire, with children forming competitive cliques called 'cutting clubs'. The more young people do it, the more their peers become curious to try it.

There is a complex mixture of reasons why young people self-harm, say experts. Seldom is there one single event that triggers it. Rather it is a build-up of helplessness, hopelessness and a general low mood. The forms it takes can be so unexpected that they are completely invisible, says Rachel Welch of selfharm.co.uk. She has come across girls who deliberately wear shoes that are too small and who keep sharp objects in their vaginas. Even promiscuity – in which a young woman repeatedly allows her body to be used – can be another way to express despair.

Boys also self-harm, as the NHS figures show. But they are less likely to come forward because it's seen as a female issue. With young men, it also takes on a different character – self-bruising, punching walls or getting into fights. While boys are less likely to turn their anger inwards, as girls do to keep up the pretence of being 'perfect', they are more likely to find expression through alcohol, playing violent games, and internet porn.

Rachel stresses that self-harm affects all sections of society. She sees as many self-harmers at schools in special measures as at top-performing institutions. 'You have underachieving children doing it and people who are going to Oxbridge. The one thing they have in common is that at the moment they are doing it, the physical pain is preferable to some of the emotional stuff that is going on.'

While self-harm is not new, Rachel believes that the strain is more intense for today's children: 'It used to be that there was a bit of pressure about what pencil case you had. If you were really lucky you had a Walkman. Now it's all about what model phone you have and how many followers you have on Facebook and Twitter.'

PARENTS AND PEERS
PRESSURE FROM ALL SIDES

IT CAN BE PARTICULARLY difficult for bewildered parents, who feel they have given their children all the love and security in the world, to accept when children start to cave in under the pressure. When there are no visible causes for mental health issues – like divorce or a chaotic home-life – at first they may see the symptoms as laziness, weakness and, later, typical teenage rebellion. This may make them hesitant to get help.

Psychologists like Madeleine Levine have found that middle-class children are particularly at risk. In fact rather than insulating children against anxiety, coming from a wealthy background appears to make children more vulnerable. She found that thirty to forty per cent of twelve- to eighteen-year-olds from wealthy backgrounds have worrying psychological symptoms.

She describes the phenomenon of middle-class parents who seem to be hovering over their children but at the same time are 'everywhere and nowhere'. While being very vigilant about their children's academic performance, they somehow miss out on their emotional needs. Because middle-class parents feel they give their children 'everything', they tend to expect more back. They also expect a return on their investment.

She says: 'While we don't know how much our parenting affects our children, parenting is the only thing we have control over. The genesis of this has to do with parents who are feeling too fragile to be able to tolerate their kids' unhappiness.'

Levine believes the problem is this: 'We are overly concerned with "the bottom line", with how our children "do" rather than with who our children are.'

Yet parents are just one part of the jigsaw puzzle.

American psychologist Suniya Luthar of Arizona State University has also studied why privileged young people have been more vulnerable than previous generations for the last decade. Similarly to Levine's, her research has found that children coming from homes with an annual income of more than £100,000 a year were suffering anxiety and depression at twice the normal rate of their less well-off peers.

Although parents often want too much from their children, the same message is being driven home just as hard by teachers, coaches and children's peers. Deanne Jade of the National Centre for Eating Disorders believes it's a complex picture. Although pushy mothers have taken the blame for eating disorders, particularly anorexia, she says it's not as simple as that. 'By nature people with eating disorders are already extra competitive because they score highly on the character trait we call social comparison.

'But social media has made things much worse. Pressure on its own is not too hurtful. What is hurtful is pressure in the face of unattainable expectations, which is the curse of our age.

'It leads to unhappiness – and unhappiness which will affect those with mental health deficits more readily. We tend not to take notice of this in early childhood. But in adolescence it will take the shape of eating disorders and risky behaviour.'

Jade says children have always developed their own idea of what qualities it is important for them to have, like being pretty, clever, popular or sporty. 'But today, there are too many areas to compete in and the bar is set too high. It means more and more there are often shortfalls between who children think they are – and who they think they should be.'

THE RISE IN TEENAGE SUICIDES

M OST ALARMING OF ALL, of course, has to be the rise in teenage suicide rates. In the UK, suicide is the second most common cause of death among fifteen- to nineteen-year-olds after road traffic accidents. Across the world, it is estimated that around a million young people try to commit suicide every year. More than 164,000 succeed, according to World Health Organisation statistics.

While there are many reasons young people kill themselves, Alastair Sharp, Deputy Director of the Samaritans in Hong Kong, believes that test-focused education 'must take some of the blame for inducing psychological problems'.

In a study of more than 6,000 English students, commissioned by the Samaritans, he said worries about stress and schoolwork came top of the list of the concerns of those feeling suicidal or who had self-harmed – ahead of bullying and relationship problems. Similar results have been found around the world. He believes it's time to move on from schooling that actively encourages performance pressure.

'Moving away from measurement-driven instruction to a more humanistic view of education ideals would help. In this view, teaching the young to live happier and healthier lives, while promoting intellectual and emotional development, is what matters.'

HELPING CHILDREN TO REACH THEIR POTENTIAL

JUST TO CLARIFY, THIS is not a book about 'finding excuses' for children not to work at their education. Children still need to reach their potential – but parents need to help them to find and achieve it in a balanced way and without suffering emotional harm.

These days many parents have come to see themselves as the 'tiger in the tank' driving their children's success. But young people will go further if they find the power to drive themselves – and will be better equipped to handle the knocks and scrapes along the way. If we want to look at where our children are heading, it's worth looking at where they are starting out from in today's education system.

WHAT'S ON OFFER FOR THE PRESCHOOL CHILD

WALK INTO ANY BRANCH of a Crème de la Crème kindergarten in the US, and you might think you have wandered into Disneyland. The main drag is a mini Victorian high street, painted in pastel colours and decked out in twinkling lights. The scaled-down boutiques are decorated with quaint, old-fashioned shop signs – in French – and have animatronic toys in the windows.

Most of the branches of Crème de la Crème, spread across nine American states, look like this. The quaint little streets are actually constructed inside giant warehouses, and the shopfronts are facades for 'enrichment' classrooms for subjects that include Spanish and Computer Science. Every half-hour, groups of preschool children are rotated between subjects. They also have the chance to pretend to be TV anchors and present their own news items and weather reports on a giant screen.

It may feel eerily fake. But Crème de la Crème has been dubbed 'mini-university' for the preschooler set. Here parents are told that their children will be given all the tools they need to excel in life. When these pint-sized students move on at the age of four or five, they don't just get to graduate with mortarboards and gowns – they also get a prom. As Cathy Brown, Services Director at one of the firm's Georgia branches, explains: 'Most of them will be going to top-tier private schools and will be at the head of their classes. They are confident and ready for the next step.'

As Glenn Doman showed, trends in education often start in America and spread to Europe. All over Britain, hothousing nurseries are mushrooming as well. Where once kindergartens were called after nursery-rhyme characters, now they have names like Clever Tots and Little Einsteins.

The settings in this country may be missing some of the twee details. But the talk here is also of assessment trackers, and learning journeys. Some nurseries have dedicated black-and-white play zones for babies to help them focus better – after all, why stick to board books when you can decorate a whole room in two-tone? Mini-sized tables and chairs get labelled in unrecognisable foreign languages, probably more for the benefit of the parents than the oblivious infants.

The Peter-and-Jane-style typefaces on the websites barely mask the underlying ambition. Before they have even turned two, toddlers are assigned specific areas of learning and development, including 'literacy' and 'maths'.

At one private nursery in North London, five years' worth of exam results are posted to show how successful the school is at getting its pupils into the capital's most impenetrable private schools. For those parents thinking even further into the future, it adds: 'It is exciting to know that at least nine ex-pupils have been offered places at Oxbridge for September.'

Sending your child to schools like these is like taking out insurance. The pot of gold at the end of this educational rainbow is a top university and a sought-after professional career. In years gone by, most children and their parents would not even start considering tertiary education until Year Eleven. Now ambitious nurseries, like this one, are where the first domino gets tipped over.

It would be easy to dismiss all this as something that happens in the private sector. But in the state sector, playing cafés in the home corner and finger painting are no longer deemed to be sufficient preparation for life either. These days, when a toddler proudly shows their nursery key worker a drawing, it won't just be accepted with a smile. It will be assessed for its developmental import and filed in a plastic folder. This is the so-called Nappy Curriculum, or Early Years Foundation Stage, compulsory for all nurseries, preschools and childminders since 2008.

It all starts gently enough, with checks on whether a very young child 'is becoming aware of how to negotiate the space and objects around them', 'can communicate their physical needs for things such as food and drink' or 'can let adults know when they are uncomfortable'. But the pace quickens. There are sixty-nine centrally set 'early learning goals'. By five, children are expected not only to be able to count up to twenty, but also to show that they can solve number problems and understand concepts such as halving and doubling.

Even after the curriculum was watered down in 2012, critics said it still put too much emphasis on getting three- and four-year-olds to perform desk-bound activities like writing, spelling and maths when they have not even officially started school – which happens in the UK at five, already the earliest start in Europe. But as one education minister put it, you don't want toddlers 'running around with no sense of purpose'.

On the contrary: early development specialists and those who actually work with children say you do. They point out that nursery-age tots are not built to be quiet, sit still, keep their hands to themselves and be patient at all times. Children need to move, play, be adventurous – and use their entire bodies to learn.

But does getting kids off to an early start actually help later on? Kathy Hirsh-Pasek, Professor of Psychology and Director of the Infant Language Laboratory at Temple University in Philadelphia, compared children in academically focused preschools with those in non-academic nurseries.

By the age of five, the children at the more academic school knew more letters and numbers. However, the advantage had faded away by the time they were six. The children from the more high-pressure schools were also found to be less keen to learn and less imaginative.

Though not widely discussed, much of the intention behind the government's drive for early education is to catch children from deprived backgrounds, who arrive at school nearly a year behind their peers from middle-income homes, according to the Sutton Trust. Ministers complain that a third of children start school proper without even basic language skills. But they are unlikely to be the same children who are enrolled in Talking Tots sign-language classes at the age of one, or who have a mother and father for whom parents' evening is the most eagerly anticipated date on the calendar.

Intensive focus in the classroom is required to give extra help to those who don't get it at home. But at the same time this ends up holding a magnifying glass over the middle-class children already placed under the microscope by their parents. Imposed, standardised curricula also gloss over the fact that nursery is already taxing for youngsters who are developmentally not yet ready to sit still and concentrate at desks for long periods of time. After all, if a child still can't use a toilet on their own, are they really going to be able to sit still and finish a worksheet?

Given the cloud of anxiety hovering over them, no wonder some of these children come to perceive education as stressful. Instead of rushing out at the end of a nursery session, excited about learning, parents find children coming home bewildered and overstimulated.

Children start comparing themselves with their peers at around the age of five, say child psychologists. By seven, any teacher will tell you that every pupil knows exactly where they come in class and what stream they are in, no matter how many ways their study tables are colour-coded. In this context, careful assessments are useful for catching those children with severe deprivation issues or developmental delays. But just as the IQ test – which was developed to spot the children who needed the help the most – has been transmuted into a way to grade entire populations, so have nursery and primary-school assessments become used to pigeonhole children.

A little boy from any background who believes he's bad at maths at age five won't get the message that it's just as important that he knows how to build a multi-layered Lego spaceship. A small girl who can't yet extract the nugget of meaning from a comprehension passage is unlikely to believe it when she's told that it's just as impressive that she's able to ride her bike without stabilisers. Both these children may be slightly later developers, and could well flourish later. But in this system, early developers get favoured and late bloomers sidelined.

Failure can become a self-fulfilling prophecy. Teachers, rushed by a succession of modules, may find it more difficult to teach children who are not developmentally ready. Often they don't have the time to repeat or embed concepts which take a little longer to grasp. In maths, if a child doesn't have the time to fully understand a complex idea such as place value, none of the operations, like addition or multiplication, which come after will make sense either.

Of course children should be challenged, but challenged a few yards beyond reach, not several miles. In the meantime, a worried child can't fail but pick up on the difference between the broad smiles the early bloomers get from teachers and teaching assistants for getting the answers right – and the disappointed looks they receive. Very soon children become worried that they are not among the ones that 'get it', and panic and the anxiety become self-reinforcing. Small internal voices start to whisper and insinuate: 'Maybe I am not so clever after all.'

In our rush for our children to get ahead, overzealous parents with the flimsiest grasp of child development can over-egg their children's abilities – proclaiming them 'ready for school'. If they work, they may also be attracted by the fact that school is cheaper than childcare at home or expensive private nurseries. But just because a twenty-two-month-old can count up to twenty does not mean they understand the meaning of numbers. More likely they have just committed the sequence to memory in a sing-song way, in the same way that they memorised Baa Baa Black Sheep.

Equally, just because a child can read out the words on a page, does not mean they can draw out the subtleties of meaning they need to enjoy the text – or extrapolate the subtle shades of interpretation demanded by increasingly difficult school comprehension exercises.

Imagine if you were presented with a page full of Italian and you had never properly been taught the language. Granted, you could probably sound it out – and perhaps be able to have a good guess at the meaning of a few of the words. But unless your knowledge and understanding of Italian was good, you would not enjoy the process or want to keep doing it.

That is why children who have been simply trained to robotically 'decode' letters are so often turned off reading. They may be able to sound out the words, but they are not necessarily able to comprehend the whole meaning if the sentence. The danger in pushing reading too early is that we may be asking many children to do something their brains are not ready for. One in ten children of primary school age are estimated to be affected by poor comprehension, but often this goes unnoticed.

Proper reading depends on lots of different functions of the brain – seeing, hearing, speaking and the ability to see in the mind's eye what is being talked about – working together. How quickly these all coordinate depends on myelination – the development of the sheath, or coating, of the axons that run between the neurons, or cells. When children are born the connections between the brain cells are like bare wires. This building-up of insulation – or myelination – which enables the signal to move fast along it is an ongoing process which continues until adolescence.

However, neuroscientists say the wiring necessary for reading often isn't in place until between the ages of five and seven, and later in boys than girls. Furthermore, studies dating back decades have found no clear appreciable difference in reading levels later on between children who started young compared with kids who started late. The only difference is that the earlier readers became less motivated.

When all privileged children have heard is parents praising them to the hilt for being clever in an attempt to puff up their self-confidence, the gap between what they have been told at home and what they are experiencing at school starts to widen. For some children, this leads to mistrust of their parents – and even anger that the all-powerful grown-ups in their lives can't wave a magic wand and fix the problem.

But tiger parents, attracted by – let's face it – the show-off appeal of having an early reader in the family, keep pressing their children to do it all as early as possible anyway. You only have to be part of the paranoia about what Biff and Chip book your child is on (some primaries have had to stop using plastic reader folders because parents were constantly checking out what level their child's classmates were on) to see how much we parents want to turn it into a race. But a race to where exactly?

At moments like this, we would do well to remember the old fable of the tortoise and the hare. There's no point having a child who is taking home level-twelve reading books in Year One, if by Year Four they are so turned off reading they never want to read on their own again. Most likely, part of the reason children of this age don't want to move beyond the Wimpy Kid books, which are broken up with cartoon drawings and have lines of text spaced far apart, is because they have been turned off huge wodges of texts introduced earlier than they could cope with.

Higher up the education system, just because children can recite times tables by rote does not mean they are ready to apply them to long division. Algebra is a subject that is being taught at a younger and younger age in schools, even though some kids simply have not had the time to develop the higher abstract brain processes it demands. If it's introduced before children have completely mastered basic arithmetic, then it's a morale-killer.

Subconsciously they may become 'fearful learners' or opt out in order not to put themselves on the line again. These children not only feel inferior. They may also develop what psychologists call 'learned helplessness' – a type of 'poor me' syndrome. When children feel they have no control over their school achievement – and nothing they do seems to makes any difference – far from fighting, they may give up trying. To the adult eye, they may appear lazy and 'not bothered'. But as former head teacher Noël Janis-Norton says: 'They are often children who have tried just one too many times – and failed.'

HOW LEAGUE TABLES HAVE CHANGED OUR SCHOOLS

O N A WARM SUMMER's day one August, during what is known in newspapers as the 'silly season', the education correspondent of the *Daily Telegraph*, John Clare, arrived at his office – and wondered what he was going to write that day.

Filling the news pages at that quiet time of the year is a challenge for all journalists, let alone education correspondents stuck in the middle of the long school holidays and the parliamentary recess.

Clare had just been at a meeting with two heads of leading private schools at which they had trumpeted the good news about their A-level results. But beneath the bragging, what was the truth, he wondered? Was there a way of finding out if they were exaggerating their success?

With time on his hands, Clare started ringing round other head teachers he knew and asking them how many of their exams had been graded A or B, reasoning that these were the grades that parents would want to know about because they were the ones which got children into university.

The results were an eye-opener. Clare recalled later: 'The figures in front of me showed that schools which I (and countless parents) had been led to believe were academic high-flyers were nothing of the sort. Conversely, many with quite modest academic profiles had stunning results.' Intrigued, he phoned 100 schools and listed them in order of their percentages of top grades. And on 29 August 1991, the *Daily Telegraph* published the first ever school league table.

Parents were transfixed. Schools, especially those that did not perform as well as their reputation suggested, were mortified. But the Tory government of the time seized on them as such a good idea that they decided to create league tables for state schools too, as a way to banish complacency and shine a searchlight on sinking schools and poor teaching.

However, although they were meant to rank institutions, more than twenty years later league tables have come to be used to rank children. The result has been to turn our schools into giant testing centres. Head teachers have become like the chairmen of public companies, judged on their fluctuating stocks and shares. Pupils are their commodities and the maximum profit must be squeezed out of them.

Educators such as Dr Martin Stephen, former High Master of St Paul's School, have gone as far as to call league tables 'a monster, eating away at some of the best things in education'. They have, he continued, 'encouraged us to turn our children into exam junkies, and reduced innovation and creativity in the classroom by creating a climate of fear among teachers.'

As for the claim that they chivvy schools out of bad performance, he added: 'They might indeed spot the survivor in the sea, but instead of handing over a life-jacket, they hold their head under water.'

Former deputy head teacher Elizabeth Cook has also bemoaned how SATs scoring, also used to draw up primary league tables, has filtered down into the playgrounds of junior schools and changed the way children think about themselves and school: 'In the playground, all the talk is about what each child scored in their tests. It's all: "She got a three", or "He's got a level two" which is average for Key Stage One, when the child is six to seven years old. But now parents get a bit disappointed if their child doesn't get a three.'

The result is that schools have become as pushy as parents, and vice versa, creating a self-reinforcing combination which is frightening for children of all ages.

Now they are such an integral part of our education system, it's easy to assume that school league tables are a fact of life globally. But Britain is in fact relatively rare. Most countries, even high-performing ones like Japan and Canada, don't have them.

The message children get from all this is that learning is not about immersing themselves in a subject. It's about cramming enough information into their skulls for the next test lurking around the corner. The result is that children become treated not so much as individuals but as footsoldiers to triumph over other youngsters in other parts of the country, and ultimately the world.

It was when I first saw my daughter's Year Seven curriculum in her first week at her comprehensive secondary school that I saw the sheer volume of testing – in subjects I didn't even know could be tested. When I was at school, the main mark of whether you were a good netball player was whether you could get the ball away from your opponent and help get it into the goal at the right end of the court. Nowadays, as well as half-term assessments in all her academic subjects, a giant green spreadsheet tells me she will get a netball skills test and fitness test. She will also be assessed on 'sequence work' and asked to write a self-evaluation on the subject.

In her dance class, in which she will be taught hip-hop, she will also be judged on developing 'a motif through devices'. Of course, curriculum areas have to be covered and levels have to be reached. But nowhere is there a box to tick for 'learning for the sake of it'.

TESTING TIMES

HOW SCHOOLS HAVE BECOME MORE ABOUT TESTING THAN ABOUT LEARNING

IN CHARLIE'S CLASS, MATHS lessons are not so much a subject as a daily race to the finish line. 'In lessons, the teachers are always encouraging us to do it faster,' says Charlie, sixteen, who decided to take Maths A level after getting a good GSCE result, but is now wondering if she made the right decision. 'I prefer to look things up in maths. I enjoy taking my time to solve equations. But in lessons, you're always being set timed work against the clock. You look up and there are always the quicker ones who have finished before you. It's demoralising.'

As the curriculum becomes increasingly obsessed with efficient exam performance, maths contests and races are becoming a daily event for our children. Recently I visited my younger daughter's school to be told about how much maths had changed since my day – and how parents could support their children at home. True, there is no better way of finding out if a child knows their times tables than by testing them. Nothing concentrates the mind better than being asked to stand in front of the teacher and recite your times tables. But it struck me that her classroom looked more like the set of a quiz show. The tables were laid with buzzers, timers and beat-your-opponent games such as maths snap. Increasingly it seems that lessons are becoming more about testing, and less about teaching.

The difficulties can start for pupils when maths becomes turned into a race before the child has even mastered the basics of the subject. Pupils who don't flourish in this adrenalin-soaked atmosphere can become test-phobic. Perhaps it's no surprise to learn that there's more talk than ever among educators about 'maths anxiety' – believed to affect more than two million school children in England alone.

Dr Dénes Szűcs, from Cambridge University's Department of Experimental Psychology, believes this may be the reason why only seven per cent of pupils in the UK study maths at A level, and why the number of students taking it at degree level is falling.

As adults, many of us will recognise the sheer panic we feel when confronted with having to work out credit card interest or mortgage rates on the spot. Yet we forget that this mind-blanking reaction often has its roots in childhood. And more than just being an intense dislike of maths or not having a natural 'maths brain', studies are finding out that maths anxiety has a biological basis.

Researchers at Stanford University studied the brain activity patterns of seven- and eight-year-olds who were worried about maths. When they asked the children to answer a set of questions, they found that their brains showed patterns similar to people with other phobias, such as about spiders. They had more brain activity in regions associated with fear, and less activity in the regions involved in problem-solving, making it even harder for them to come up with the right answers.

Dr Vinod Menon, the professor who led the project, told the *Guardian*: 'Our research is important…because it shows that math anxiety in children is real. It cannot be wished away. It needs to be attended to and treated if it persists.'

Jenny Foster, who has treated children with maths anxiety, says: 'Unfortunately our brains do not discriminate between real and imagined danger. If a child feels anxious or fearful about imminent testing or worried or humiliated about one aspect of learning, the reptilian brain takes over and it become impossible to think at higher levels.

'When we hear someone tell us, even though they revised thoroughly, their mind went blank when they turned over a test paper, they are literally describing their experience. That fight-or-flight response was useful for our cavemen ancestors when they had to flee from a mountain lion.

'But in a school setting, the section of the brain which needs to be engaged when answering test questions effectively shuts down. While a little bit of nerves is fine, in these children the brain makes no distinction between real danger and imaginary – and in a test situation that's s not helpful.'

Yet many teachers take the view that constantly exposing children to maths drills and tests will 'get them used to it'. The theory is that the more they do quick-fire tests, the less anxious they will become. If anything, the opposite is true. While timed challenges are useful for helping children recall facts faster and more automatically, they won't work for the pupils who don't understand what they are being quizzed on in the first place. They punish the pupils who still need time to work out the answers – and who are by now so anxious that they are even less able to do so. The more wrong answers they get, the more they believe they can't do it. Moreover, timed tests mean that the few children who do 'get it' are constantly rewarded for their success.

Maths is a particularly sensitive area, not only because it is where much of the emphasis of the new curriculum lies. It's also a subject about which children tend to think in black and white. They assume they are either 'good' or 'bad' at it. Once those labels are in place, it can be difficult to shift them.

HOW TIGER PARENTING AFFECTS OUR RELATIONSHIP WITH OUR CHILDREN

PERHAPS FEWER MOTHERS AND fathers would start high performance parenting with babies and toddlers if they realised how much resentment it creates in their children later on.

The cruel irony of all this stress, panic and intensive effort on our offspring's behalf is that it pushes away the very people we are trying to protect. While all of us would say we love our children no matter how well they do, unfortunately that's not the message children always hear – and that is what matters. Instead, children become angry at their sense of powerlessness when they feel we are turning them into passive projects.

Even as toddlers, children can work out when they are being played with because you simply want to be with them, and when you are playing with them to teach them something. At the same time, parents can feel so instrumental to a child's success that they may not realise how much they are claiming their offspring's achievements as their own.

I clearly remember an open day at my child's school when an over-involved mother pointed to a piece of artwork – an Egyptian-style scroll – on the wall. It was supposed to have been done by her daughter, but the mother proclaimed 'I did that' for half the room to hear. No doubt – in the sincere hope of helping her daughter do the best history project – she had lovingly soaked the paper in tea herself to make it look like papyrus. But the look of bewilderment and humiliation on her daughter's face was heartbreaking.

So often perfectly articulate children are also spoken for by their parents in their presence, or used by adults to show off, leaving youngsters feeling stifled and, even worse, used. As with all forms of parenting, some of how this plays out will depend on the fit between the parent and child and how their temperaments complement each other. An extrovert, innately competitive child may love the fact that there are not one, but two cameras and a camera phone trained on her while she attempts the long jump on sports day. But it's also worth considering that other more constitutionally modest and introverted children may feel acutely self-conscious and inhibited by the overwhelming attention.

The problem is that for most of their childhoods children cannot speak out about what is making them uncomfortable. At first they may not even be able to pinpoint how they feel. But nevertheless, the more sensitive ones soon cotton on to the fact that their achievements are being commandeered by adults – and claimed as personal victories. A child of eight cannot turn around to his parents and say: 'Is the real reason you are asking me to do this because it makes you look good?'

When the little girl I described heard her mother announcing that she had done her project, was she really in a position to respond in public to the woman who was the source of all her emotional and physical security? Lost in a haze of humiliation and confusion, she was speechless.

Younger children are so dependent on adults that they cannot allow themselves to openly express their resentment – driving it underground into hostility, detachment or rebellion. They cannot afford to have feelings of hatred. But eventually, when they are old enough to start detaching themselves, they may seek to control their destinies away from their parents with behaviour that is out of their control – such as self-harm or eating disorders.

Ultimately, competitive parenting strikes at the very core of the child-parent bond because children come to believe that their parents love them more when they do well – and less when they don't.

In one 2004 study by motivational psychologists, 100 college students were asked if they felt loved more by their mothers and fathers if they succeeded at school. It was found that children who had conditional approval were more likely to do what their parents wanted. But these students were also more likely to resent their parents because they felt rejected when they did poorly and they therefore grew to dislike them. The students' own joy at their success was also fleeting, perhaps because they were brought up to please others, not themselves.

A further study by the University of Denver found that teens who had to meet certain standards to win their parents' approval were less likely to like themselves. Instead it led to them creating 'a false self' and pretending to be the person their families wanted. Overall, children who feel liked by their parents for who they are tend to accept and like themselves more.

Even though they cannot be verbally expressed, these feelings of resentment can also start young. Researchers at the University of Missouri found that when mothers took control of young children's playtime, the children showed more negative feelings towards them.

The psychologist Oliver James has also observed in his work that parents who make their love conditional on performance tend to depress their children – because to them it feels like their best is never good enough. It is, he says, 'a distortion of power and size'.

As parents we have to ask ourselves some frank questions: Do we smile and love and hug our children just a little bit more when they reflect well on us and when their achievements make us look good? Are we a little bit more reserved when we feel they have let us down? Even if the difference is only superficial, children pick up on the message loud and clear: 'I am loved not for who I am, but for what I do.' The most destructive love is love that has to be earned.

REAL-LIFE EXPERIENCES

'My mother didn't speak to me for a week after I got my A level results because I didn't get any As…I made it to university anyway but the message I got loud and clear was I was only as good as my last exam result. I still carry around a lot of resentment against my parents.'

Penny, 25

'Getting into Oxbridge was traumatic for me because of my pushy mother who just enjoyed bragging about it. When I tried to take an overdose, she accused me of embarrassing her. She treated me better when I did well in exams. The result was that I worked harder to win her love. When I had a mental breakdown, she accused me of trying to get my own way. I hate her guts now because now I realise she didn't love me, she just loved my achievements.'

Kate, 35

HOW COMPETITION AFFECTS
RELATIONSHIPS BETWEEN CHILDREN

MOLLY AND HER BEST friends have sat on the top maths table since Year One. Of course, their form teacher would never *say* they are in the top maths set. She just calls it the yellow table. But the five children who sit there have got the message loud and clear – and they want everyone else in the class to know it too.

If Molly, a competitive 8-year-old who has been encouraged by her parents to believe she is the best, happens to catch sight of another child working on an easier page in their class workbook, she whispers and giggles to her friends next to her.

When the teacher left the room the other day to speak to a colleague, Molly saw her chance – and craned her neck enough to be able to spot the fact that Sophie on the orange table was doing a four-times-table worksheet. Molly and her friend had been set work to practise their twelves. Spotting her opportunity, Molly announced: 'I can't believe you're only on that' in front of the rest of the class, causing the rest of the class to look round. Sophie fled to the toilet in tears.

Further up the school in Year Six, Amy, Daniella, Phoebe and Chloe are among the group also clearly favoured to do well in Maths in the upcoming 11-plus. Indeed, the teacher makes no secret of the fact that they are the select, gifted few. Moreover, she believes that setting the group up as an example will motivate the rest. In class, she tells the favoured group to 'knock [the other pupils'] socks off' with their correct answers.

In what was once a happy and harmonious classroom, this has created a tense atmosphere and a 'them and us' attitude. When another pupil asked Phoebe, the most superior of the group, for help during a team exercise, she replied: 'I'm afraid you'll just have to work that out for yourself, won't you?'

And so it goes on up the school. In Year Eleven, when the teacher announces that there will be review of equilateral equations because some students are not secure with them, Amelia, who always sits in the front row, comments so the rest of the class will hear: 'I can't believe some people still don't get them.'

When children first start school, they are happily unaware of how they compare with their classmates. But, encouraged by parents and a competitive school system, which still believes that children can be shamed into working harder, they soon catch on.

Competitive parenting does not fly over our children's heads. If we raise them from the start to see life as a contest over everything, from who walks first to who has the most advanced reading book, even small children soon catch on. If the first question we ask them when they come out of the school gates is not just 'What did you get in your spelling test?' but also 'What did everyone else get?' then it's no surprise that kids soon learn to measure their achievements not in their own right, but by comparison to others.

Because only one child can truly be the winner by beating the rest, competition creates hostility. The more the winners win, the more rewarded they are by schools who shower them with titles, prizes and public praise. The more the losers lose, the more they view the victors as 'favourites' who are unassailable.

Competition can pervade children's relationships early. Friendships tend to be defined by status. The contest for who is the oldest, prettiest or the best at drama or music starts to organize our classrooms.

Often close rivals will stick together, not only because they are more alike in personality, but also because it pays to keep an eye on their closest opponent as they vie for the top spot. And children will end up pressing each other's buttons, particularly if they have been set against each other by their parents in competition for the same prize.

Among little girls, who are socialised to try and avoid out-and-out conflict, this may surface in snide comments, exclusion, gossip, lying and inflation of their own achievements to try to keep their opponents in the subordinate position. Rivalries between boys are less common in the playground, as they can play it out in sport – although it can come to the fore fiercely between brothers.

Competition not only puts pressure on existing friendships; it also stops them forming in the first place. Just like adults in the workplace, other less confident children may keep their distance from potential rivals in case next week they happen to come up against each other.

As children move up the school, classrooms can become unhappy places, split into cliques formed on the basis of who is better than whom – and at what. The areas over which children will compete will expand into who is the best dressed, the most socially influential, and who's the first to get a boyfriend or girlfriend. It is often at this point that less academically successful children get their payback, as they are likely to be seen as cooler and less nerdy.

You may consider that this has always been the politics of the playground. But researchers are finding that judgemental attitudes are being sharpened by the steady stream of competitive reality TV programmes which make up our regular viewing. Competition over everything from who can lose weight the fastest to who bakes the best cakes has come to dominate UK entertainment schedules. With some shows attracting up to 14 million viewers, children and teens have become their biggest consumers.

Although these pre-watershed programmes are seen as 'family entertainment', psychologists and teachers are becoming increasingly worried about their effect on young people. There may not be the shoot-outs and kung-fu kicks that there once were before 9 p.m. Instead the physical blows have been replaced by put-downs, sulking, eye-rolling and bullying – dressed up by glossy sets and designer clothes.

In fact, on closer analysis, in a study by Brigham Young University in the US researchers found that reality TV features on average eighty-five verbal attacks, insults or snide remarks every hour – almost twice the number seen in comedies, dramas or even soaps.

The result is that in a competitive society, kids become professional mini-critics. Being judge and jury – and then posting your verdicts on social networks – has become a new way to claw back a fleeting sense of self-worth.

Parents who try to breed competition in their children do them no favours. Children start to learn that it feels good when others fail. Furthermore, training your child to compete with others means that failure, when it comes, will damage your son's or daughter's self-worth far more than it needs to. For one thing, they know that by going public, you have staked your reputation on their success. They also know that their classmates are gloating because that's what they've done to others. Instead of feeling just bruised when they trip up, they feel mortally wounded.

HOW COMPETITIVENESS RUINS OUR EXPERIENCE OF PARENTING

REMEMBER WHEN YOU AND your partner were expecting your first baby? Did you look forward to playing with, cuddling and just enjoying your child? Do you recall when every scribble was a masterpiece, every new word a delight, every step a minor miracle?

And then the comparisons started.

One of the most miserable things about competitive parenting is that unless we consciously confront how it makes us feel, child-rearing turns into one, long miserable game of one-upmanship. The fact is that as well as amplifying the already huge pressures on kids, tiger parenting is not much fun for you either. When we measure our children against their peers, we stop appreciating our children for who they are. We give up enjoying our offspring in their own right and start becoming fixated on their achievements instead.

Since the earliest days of those first fictional pushy mothers, Mrs Bennet and Mrs Worthington, competitive parenting has been depicted as a selfish desire to bask in our children's glories. Tiger parents have been accused of everything under the sun, from egotism to rampant narcissism.

It's so much more complicated than that, though. True, there is a hard core of pathologically obsessed parents – about five per cent – who give pushy parenting a bad name. But really most so-called tiger parents are people who simply want their children to reach their potential so they can look after themselves in life – but have got carried way.

Most so-called pushy parenting starts from a place of love. The protectiveness a mother or father feels for their child is one of the most primal instincts we have. When we first bring this perfect, helpless person into the world, we hold the highest hopes and aspirations for them. But it's a role which also taps into our deepest insecurities and unlocks our anxieties. In our effort to find out if we are doing the best job we can, we measure both ourselves and our children against others outside our family.

The closer we are to others, the more likely we are to experience feelings of envy. There's not much closer you can get than when you live in the same area, your kids are the same age and you send them to the same schools. Education starts out as a level playing field so the comparisons can be very stark. In a modern capitalist society where we are judged to be solely responsible for our own successes – and by extension those of our children – failure has become even more crushing.

Once we could put it all down the will of God. Now it's all up to us. The result is that we do everything we can to try to avoid falling short – especially when it comes to a job as important as parenting.

HOW COMPETITIVE PARENTING HARMS ADULT FRIENDSHIPS AND RELATIONSHIPS

As ADULTS, WE MAY feel we have learnt to cope with failure and rejection. But when these are visited on our child, they feel much worse – more like a 1,000-volt shock from a cattle prod. Whether it's making the soccer team or getting into a school, we are not only tormented that someone does not consider our child good enough. More than that, we instantly turn it back on ourselves – and wonder what we did wrong to cause our child to be rejected. The buffeting our children can get in the competitive education system means that few children succeed all the time – and even the most confident parent can lose their nerve and wonder if they have let their child down.

It was psychologist Dr Wendy Grolnick who coined the phrase

'pressured parent syndrome' to describe 'the visceral anxiety triggered when the ever-increasing competition – academic, athletic, social, or artistic – that our kids face today switches on our psychological hard-wiring'.

Today's hothouse is so overheated that unless we check ourselves, that fear that our child is under threat and the resulting pain make us do things we never thought we'd do – as well as have feelings we don't recognise or like in ourselves.

In today's sink-or-swim society, the sad truth is that we are more likely to feel panicked by the achievements of other people's children than pleased by them, making us feel mean-spirited and nasty. Even though our own offspring may be blissfully oblivious at first, our knee-jerk reaction when we see another youngster doing something more impressive is to wonder why ours can't do the same.

Lillian remembers when a friend with a son the same age came to see her child play a solo cello piece at a concert. 'I thought at the time it was strange that she should make the effort to see Milo play at such short notice. At the time I was really rather touched. After his piece, my friend was very complimentary about Milo's performance. Then I happened to see that she had been straight on her phone to text her son's own cello teacher to ask what could be done to get her child up to the same standard.'

Another mother, Belinda, describes the 'one finger clap' she uses to describe the grudging applause in school concerts for performers who are more competent than her son. Other mothers admitted to feigning disinterest, looking bored or saying as little as possible.

Denise recalls: 'I remember being at my friend's house and putting on a CD that my son Alex had sung on for a charity concert and that was going to be released. The couple were really good friends of ours through our children, so I genuinely wanted them to hear it, not to show off. I just wanted to share what a lovely song it was.

'But when I played it, I just got virtual silence and barely even polite interest. I quickly got the message loud and clear that I should have kept it to myself. It was so disappointing to get it from a close friend who I thought loved my child too. That's what hurts most. At moments like that, you feel that you are on your own.'

Ultimately such begrudging behaviour forms the start of a chain reaction. The more mean-spirited other parents are about our children, the more mean-spirited we become about theirs. When a genuine, heart-felt compliment becomes hard to give, it's then that otherwise decent people realise they too have become infected. Gail says she knew that moment had come when she viewed another mother's Facebook page.

'There was a friend of mine posting about how her son had been able to write his name for the first time – with a picture – as if we should all be impressed. I had to admit my hand really hovered over the 'Like' button – because my son was still some way off that point. So I ignored it.

'I know it happens the other way around too. When my ten-year-old daughter won a singing competition, I was just so proud I couldn't stop myself posting her performance. I could see that fifteen other parents on my Facebook page viewed it – but not one 'liked' it. But a few days later, I did notice some really bitchy, sarcastic comments between two mums about how they needed to start their children on singing lessons soon if they wanted to train up the next Adele.'

The intensity of emotions at moments like these can be shocking. Dawn remembers a moment when her two-year-old daughter and her best friend – born just a few weeks apart – were playing in the sand pit. She recalls: 'Suddenly Rachel's friend came out with a complete sentence: "I want to go on the swings." All my daughter could say at the time was "swing". At that moment, I wanted to trip the other child up. I felt so ashamed of myself afterwards – but that sudden terror that my child wasn't up to scratch ambushed me.'

In the course of researching this book, I found that very few mothers will admit to these feelings openly. For the most part, competitive parenting has become hidden and taboo. In our society, mothers in particular are supposed to care for and feel protective of all children. It feels unnatural to say that we only want our children to win – and to leave the competitors trailing in the dust. We are not supposed to feel so insecure and vulnerable. To admit such a feeling would be an admission that we fear our children are, indeed, lacking something. We are far too ashamed of our angst to ever admit it. Few parents will come out and say 'I am so furious that my child hasn't been moved up to the first violin in the school orchestra that I am spitting blood' – even if they feel it.

Pushy mothers are such objects of derision that we've all got the message that's it not good to act like one. But it does not stop us experiencing those feelings fiercely – and then feeling guilty about them. It means that competitive parenting gets driven underground, leading to a cloak-and-dagger culture of secrecy that is no fun for anyone. Even close friends don't share information. Elizabeth recalls: 'For three years, I was best friends with Donna. She was always making out her eldest son was exceptionally bright and I believed her. It was only when her old nanny came to work for me that I found that Donna's mother, who is an ex-primary school head teacher, was coming to tutor him *three* times a week. But I wasn't supposed to know that. It was all supposed to look so effortless.'

Instead parents find themselves behaving like secret service operatives; volunteering to help on school trips because they want to see how other children behave and fill in their museum worksheets – and rifling through school bags on playdates to check the marks in the visiting children's exercise books.

Anna admits she turns her wooden file of her son's Bond workbooks to the wall when other parents come round, lest they realise how much effort she is putting into helping him. She says: 'Once my son's tutor arrived when another mother was still here and I could have cringed with embarrassment. Not only did I not want the other mother to know Andrew was getting help. I also knew it would spread through the class and the other mums would get one too.'

HOW SCHOOLS TURN UP THE
TEMPERATURE

N OT SURPRISINGLY, TIGER PARENTING is whipped to a frenzy by the contest to get into good schools.

Many parents report that they were unprepared for the levels of competition they would encounter, especially when children first enter the school system. The system is manipulated by schools, who want to seem as desirable as possible to secure the best candidates – and push their league-table results higher.

Christine will never forget the moment when she asked the head of her daughter's nursery if her child had been accepted to the selective private school she had been prepping her for. Even though Amy was only just four, she had so far survived two fiercely competitive rounds, against hundreds of other candidates. Christine said: 'I knew the head would already have the results so I grabbed her at drop-off and asked her to give me the nod. She made a grimace and said: "I'm so sorry."

'I just got in my car on autopilot, drove to a lay-by and sobbed. As a first-time mum, I had stupidly got caught up in the hysteria at the school gates. There had been so much talk about who was getting in and who wasn't; this was total humiliation.

'The next day I had to listen to the mother of another girl who had been accepted just because she was a sibling say: "Well, it's so nice to know your child is bright, isn't it?" I have could have punched her. I learnt to keep my distance after that.'

Kate still remembers exactly where she was standing when she opened a school rejection letter for her four-year-old daughter. 'I felt I had been punched in the stomach. I could deal with the bullsh*t about how "it was a field of very strong candidates" if it was about me. But when it was about my child, I found it unbearable. I felt I'd hardly given birth to her and she'd already been written off. Every day, I've had to drive past the school, look at the children going in in their uniforms and think: 'So what have they got that my child hasn't?'

Some parents simply decide they don't want to put themselves or their children through it – which is why there is an exodus from competitive hotbeds leading up to key school admissions times – even if some parents don't admit that's the reason.

Jane is one of the mothers who would rather opt out than keep pushing her child. After six years raising her daughter in southwest London, she decided to move her business to the countryside. The final straw was when she tried to arrange a playdate with the mother of a classmate – and she couldn't find a slot for two months because her daughter's schedule was so packed with Kumon and extra-curricular activities.

'I just got fed up. You'd go round to pick up your child from playdates and the mums would greet you at the door with comments about what they had observed about their aptitudes. I think the competition at an early age doesn't make the children very nice either. My daughter was teased for singing a nursery rhyme by another über-sophisticated child who said it was "a baby song".

'Then there's the competition over issues like music. All you have to do is start talking about piano lessons. Suddenly the conversation goes quiet and you can hear a pin drop.'

But other parents who are tied in to where they live for economic or career reasons – or are determined to fight back so their child is never rejected again – keep battling. After all, the stakes are high. Parents can feel acutely judged according to what school their child goes to. 'There's a shorthand,' says Joanna. 'Everyone knows the academic and non-academic schools. You just have mention where your child goes, and their intelligence is instantly pegged.

'I sometimes have to steel myself to say my daughter's school name slowly, clearly and without apology – and then pinch myself not to justify it – because it's a non-selective school. Talk to parents who have a child at one of the top establishments, and they can't blurt the name out quickly enough.'

THE SCRAMBLE
FOR STATE SCHOOL PLACES

IT'S EASY TO RIDICULE parents trying to get their children into selective independent schools. But parents trying to secure a place for their children at state schools are also being driven to distraction.

Furthermore, pushy parenting can no longer be dismissed as a niche, middle-class issue. As seven out of ten people now view themselves as belonging to so-called Middle Britain, compared with a quarter a generation ago, it's much more widespread. When you consider that nearly a quarter also believe that your class is defined by your education, you can see how schools are seen as the route to upward mobility.

State-school parents may not have to cram their children through the same assessments. But they do end up pitching tents on school doorsteps to register, faking their religion and attending church, using false addresses, and even impersonating other people to get places. Every year, they are driven to the brink by the news that one in three children in places like London misses on out on their first choice – and up to thirteen children are competing for each place at the best selective state schools.

Distance from school can come down to which floor you live on in a block of flats. For the most popular schools the catchment area is down to 167 metres. Housing microclimates form as house prices rocket with a school's league table position. According to a recent Sutton Trust report, as many as a third of professional parents with children aged five to sixteen have moved to a neighbourhood for its schools. Almost a fifth have moved specifically to live in a particular catchment area.

A recent Government report admitted that an overstretched admissions system is under pressure from a rising population, forcing families with children as young as six to hire tutors to get into grammar schools.

There are 164 grammar schools left in the England, set up to help the most able top quarter of the country's pupils get the most rigorous education. On some exam days, staff have to use megaphones to keep children and parents in check. At Wallington County Grammar School in Surrey, police were once called to stop 'havoc'.

'It really can't be exaggerated how much in demand places at grammar schools are now,' says Janette Wallis of the Good Schools Guide. 'We regularly see parents who are suffering from heart palpitations, or battling with sleeping-pill dependencies because of the strain.' When surveyed, parents have compared the stress of getting their child into a school to the pain of childbirth.

There is also a rise in cheating among desperate parents. Over the last five years, the number of council investigations into suspicious school applications has risen eleven-fold. Parent turns against parent. At Eleanor Palmer School in Kentish Town, North London, some turned to spying to catch out rivals who temporarily rented accommodation inside the tiny catchment area to secure a slot. As one said: 'If you had told me a few years ago that I would be sitting in my car, attempting to covertly identify suspected school place "thieves", I wouldn't have believed you.'

Up the road in Crouch End, a mother was caught assuming the identity of a rival parent to try and get her young daughter into the area's most sought-after school. She set up an email account in the name of another mum and then asked for the child's name to be removed from the waiting list.

For secondary school, the paranoia does not stop. Parents vie to find ways to get their children labelled as 'gifted' or 'talented' so they will get special treatment – and chart their downward and upward progress through sets more intently than dealers watch the stock exchange.

'Spare me the amount of times others mums manage to slip it into conversation if they manage to get their child into the Gifted and Talented set,' says Karla. 'What does it say to the kids who aren't picked? That they are not? It seems it's never enough for your child just to be middle-of-the-road any more. In my day, it was fine to be average. Now if your child's just ordinary, you feel like a loser.'

REAL-LIFE EXPERIENCES

'The 11-plus is completely dog eat dog. It's really intense. You wouldn't believe how stressed people become. Every year, I think things can't become more manic – and they always do. On the day of the exam, you see children crying, wetting themselves, or being sick. I have to prep my children that that's what they will see and not to let it faze them.'

Stephanie Williams, Tutor, S6 Tutoring

'When Maddy was getting ready for the 11-plus, I stopped all her extra-curricular activities and told her she couldn't go to sleepovers until after the exams. I know I sound like a pushy parent but it's worth a couple of years of their childhood to set them up at a good university.'

Eva, mother of three

'I assumed that as Gemma was bright, she would sail through the 11-plus. Then she came home one day and announced she was the only child in her class not being tutored. What could I do? If I did nothing, she was going to fall behind. You need to be able to sleep at night knowing you pulled out all the stops for your child.'

Jemima, mother of two

WHAT KIND OF COMPETITIVE PARENT ARE YOU?

TIGER PARENTS CAN BE broadly divided into two breeds. Tiger parents in flight are worried that unless they push hard their child will get left behind – and their confidence will never recover. The other species is more notorious – tiger parents on the attack – determined to keep their child way ahead in a competitive world.

It may be painful at times, but I am going to challenge you to see if you have ever used any of these justifications in your tiger parenting. The aim is to help you better understand your response to the competitive pressures around you – and ask yourself if it serves either you or your children.

Most of these rationalisations are based on love, but some also owe something to fear and denial. You have probably used a mixture of these reasons to shape your parenting, but see which ones resonate with you.

Why we are tiger parents

- **'I don't want my child to be left behind':** This is the parent who doesn't want to push, but feels panicked and terrified that if their child doesn't have a tutor they will fall behind and be scarred for life. It's safe to say that many parents reading this book will fall into this category. They don't like the system, but they don't feel there's any other choice if their child is to keep their head above water.

- **'It makes me feel like a good parent':** Having a baby is a huge gamble. None of us really knows how it will turn out. But some first-time parents like to try and wrestle back control, believing that if they organise a full timetable of enrichment activities for their child from birth, then success must surely follow. These parents tend to oversimplify child-rearing. But the truth is they are simply not experienced enough to realise that there's a lot of luck involved in landing a genius child – and that education is a long game.

- **'It's tough out there'**: Life's only going to get harder, so kids had better get used to it, is the philosophy of these parents. Rather than protect their children from the high-achievement culture, they thrust them into it as soon as possible. You can spot them because they have phrases like 'work hard and play hard' written in the magnetic letters on their fridge – and can be spotted putting their primary age children through their paces at the local park in preparation for sports day.

- **'I want to belong'**: Usually mothers, these are social queen bees who build their circle by getting their children into the right nurseries and expect that the rest will follow. These parents may also be outsiders for whom having the right school uniform is a sign that they have truly arrived. They will base their decision on where to send their child on where the highest number of PLUs (people like us) can be found. They won't hesitate to take their child out of a school if they think the parents at another establishment will be more 'them'.

- **'My kids are my job'**: These are Type A parents who have given up good careers and now feel challenged to succeed in another area: parenting. Often these are mothers who were competitive in the workplace and now find it impossible to let go. Having given up considerable earning power, they run their children like companies, expecting the investment of their time and hard work to reap clear rewards.

- **'I don't want my kids to lose out because I work'**: These parents are incredibly rushed and use extra-curricular activities as a guilt-free babysitting service – and to check that their au pairs aren't parking the children in front of the TV while they are at work. Often these are creative and disorganised types who are too tired to be consistent when they get home. For this reason, they can lose out in the competitive parenting race unless they have very gifted children.

- **'I want to know I am doing the best job I can'**: A fairly recent addition to the pantheon, this is the parent who has had a good degree of success getting their children into the best schools and views it as a badge of good parenting. These mothers and fathers see no need for secrecy and feel their efforts should be acknowledged. Outgoing and outspoken, the 'competitive and proud' parent wants the world to know they have sacrificed a lot – and what's more if there were more families like them, the country wouldn't be in such a mess. Parent-in-chief in this category is Prime Minister David Cameron, who nailed his colours to the mast by announcing: 'I say it loud and proud: Samantha and I are pushy parents.'

- **'It worked for me'**: Closely related to the 'It's tough out there' types, these mums and dads tend to be high-achievers who have always thrived in competitive schools because they found it easy to do well. Often they went to Oxbridge, and believe this was vital to their life success. Now the 'It worked for me' parents want their children to have access to the same club, even though they may have different temperaments and abilities. Because these parents are so often successful, sensitive children from these families can sometimes develop inferiority complexes, and feel they can never live up to their parents' standards. They can therefore go in the other direction, with the result that these parents become ever more exasperated trying to make their offspring as successful as they are.

- **'My child must have it better than I did'**: Often new arrivals to Britain, these parents believe the only way to overcome discrimination on the grounds of race or class is to help their children secure respected professional jobs. These families have no qualms about tutoring. In fact the more they do for their offspring, the more respected they feel inside their communities.

- **'My child should achieve what I never did'**: It was psychologist Karl Jung who first pointed out: 'The greatest threat to the child is the unlived life of the mother.' These are mums and dads who never quite achieved enough in their chosen area, but know enough about it to try and push their offspring to the next level. Although they would never admit it, their child's successes also tend to make them

REAL-LIFE EXPERIENCES

'I always assumed that I would have a child as bright as me and my husband so it's been a long process to come to terms with the reality. I agonised for years wondering what had gone wrong. Was it that glass of champagne I'd had when I was pregnant with my daughter at a sensitive stage of her development in the womb? Had my stress levels during pregnancy damaged her? I tried not to compare to other children but when you are looking for them, they are hard to avoid. Whatever any one said about what a lovely child she was I felt patronised. I couldn't talk to anyone. How do you say: I am disappointed because I desperately need my child to outshine yours.'

Celia, mother of two

'At school open days, instead of appreciating my child's work, I end up scanning the stories on the walls of the other children to see who's got the most well-formed handwriting; the best use of language. It feels like more of an information gathering exercise. If my daughter had a piece of work that did not look as good as her classmates', I felt like cringing.'

Pippa, mother of one

'I don't like the idea of being a tiger mother, but what choice is there? If Dulcie goes to school with a smattering of French, Mandarin, knowing her alphabet and numbers and a few of the great composers and artists, she will arrive feeling confident. So much is expected from children nowadays that you can't sit back and do nothing. You have to get them off to the right start.'

Anna, mother of one

feel better about their own failures. Such parents can be critical because they have been through the mill themselves and take on the role of coach. Extremely thick-skinned, they tend to be invested in high-stakes areas like sport and performing arts – and will stop at nothing to make their progeny stand out.

- 'I expect my child to be gifted': These are parents who excel in areas like maths or music, where the achievements are very measurable. They tend to come from a long line of high-achievers and believe their genes alone will guarantee genius in their child. However, they can get resentful when it doesn't happen – or if other parents, who they feel aren't as entitled as they are, produce children who are more talented.

THE TACTICS OF TIGER PARENTS

NOW WE HAVE ESTABLISHED how tiger parents justify their behaviour, it's time to look at the tactics they use. It is not always a pretty picture. But if you want to shed your stripes, it pays to know how your actions are viewed by others.

The Swan

These are the 'Who me?'s of the competitive parenting world. Their approach is to affect nonchalance – and scream until they are blue in the face that they could never, never push their children. Intensely secretive, the truth is that they are passionately invested – but don't want to show their hand.

Now that competitive parenting has been driven underground, the Swan is probably the biggest tiger parent subspecies. The Swan's aim is to ensure that their children do well – but to make it look as if it's all by magic because their offspring are genetically blessed.

As brilliant actors, Swans manage to keep their motives under wraps most of the time – but the mask may slip at events like sports day. Realising that they have let their carefully crafted persona slip by going all out to win the parents' race, they immediately bounce back to proclaiming that it's 'just good fun'.

Swans are crafty and will often be complimentary about your child to throw you off the scent. They tend to be sympathetic and interested in your parenting dilemmas. But rewind the conversation and you will see that a skilled Swan will have deftly pushed your buttons to get you to let your guard down. That way they can elicit more information about how well your child is doing without giving anything away themselves.

Other clues are that they tend to be very controlling about playdates, lest they disturb the carefully organised routines at home – which they don't want you to know anything about. Last-minute arrangements are out of the question, as they need plenty of warning to hide away their library of workbooks and educational tools.

The Copy-Cat

If your child is doing well in a particular area, such as an unusual extra-curricular activity that no one has heard of, or playing a particularly impressive musical piece, lo and behold, the Copy-Cat is right behind you, signing up for same thing or buying the same music books. Usually mums, Copy-Cats carefully track your every move because they consider that you are doing something right and don't want their children to miss out.

The Spy

At the more extreme end of the spectrum, Spies are parents who are prepared to use underhand methods to find out how your child rates next to theirs – and how much of a threat they pose. These are tiger parents who will follow you from school to find out which tutor you are going to – or hand your child a worksheet on a playdate to assess their level. The Spy will use this inside knowledge either to dismiss your offspring – or to resolve to make her own children work harder in order to pull ahead.

The Music Parent

Music Parents are the ones who can't keep a straight face when your child plays during music assembly because their ten-year-old is already grade six. Music parents are mostly competitive with each other because of the high stakes involved: namely scholarships and top billings for solos at school concerts. Music parents play by another set of rules, known only to each other, based on which elite teacher they can secure and which junior academy they can get their child into.

The Pathological Parent

Thankfully in the minority, these are the man-eaters of the tiger parenting world, who give competitive parenting a *really, really* bad name. Luckily they are relatively few and far between, but they tend to be notorious. At worst, their antics end up in national newspapers. Usually overlapping with the Spy type, Pathologicals will stop at nothing, including spreading rumours about other people's children who they consider to be threats. Tactics include accusing other children of cheating, intimidating rival children on the sports field and grossly inflating their offspring's own achievements. Usually damaged as children by their own parents and chronically insecure beneath their scary exteriors, therapy is their only hope – but they are unlikely ever to seek it out. Pathologicals are best avoided at all costs as they cannot be stopped, even by their partners, who are usually bullied into submission or brainwashed into going along with it. This can only end badly, especially for their children.

The X-Factor Parent

These are the parents in the front row at every school performance, mouthing the words to solos while filming their child's performance on at least two or three digital devices. They have their children in stage schools at weekends and post everything on YouTube in the hope of turning their children into internet sensations and getting noticed by an agent.

The Humblebragger

The Humblebragger knows full well it's not cool to be seen as an out-and-out competitive parent. However, they can't help themselves and so have to find creative ways to make the point. The Humblebragger is most common among inexperienced first-time parents. A common tactic is to write posts on Facebook worrying about their child's development because they are so far ahead they are worried they might get bored. Other classics including complaining to anyone that will listen that they can't even pronounce the words in their child's (very advanced) reading book – and wondering aloud if they need to brush up on their language skills to keep up with their six-year-old who now plays Simon Says in Mandarin. The deafening lack of response from anyone else, except for grandparents, should be all the evidence they need that this doesn't go down well with other parents – but they still can't help themselves.

The Prodigy Parent

This parent is very keen that their child's talent is acknowledged – usually in areas like chess or music. Because a superhuman amount of time and money has gone into nurturing their child's 'special' gift, they become super-sensitive and demand special treatment from schools if for any reason they think their child is not being noticed. After getting off to a strong start, prodigy parents tend to find life tougher as they progress up the ladder and come across children who are more naturally talented than theirs. Prodigy parents may therefore opt to keep their child in the same school as a big fish in a small pond. They don't like any competition from anyone.

The Interrogator

Not as subtle as the Spy, Interrogators are usually mums who are so competitive and anxious that they can't keep it under wraps. To find out what level of SATs your child is working at, they will throw out a snippet of information about their own efforts in the hope that you will respond – but if that doesn't work, they will switch to direct interrogation. Their philosophy is best defined as 'keep your friends close and your enemies closer'. A typical opening gambit might be: 'Melissa is doing grade three piano. What grade are you taking next? How much is she practising?'

The Score Settler

This parent has a child who does not excel within the narrow confines of success in today's schools – and so they go all out to settle the score by training for the sports day parents' race – or by putting an excessive amount of effort into every other competition going, ranging from the Easter bonnet contest to the World Book Day dressing-up competition. Often creative and disorganised types, Score Settlers are just as competitive as others but have to use alternative methods to wreak revenge on more organised rivals. They also hope that their bursts of artistic flair will underline how dull and unimaginative everyone else is. The Score Settler will go overboard with the Cath Kidston partyware to throw the most tasteful children's parties. The tragedy is that all these efforts go unnoticed by other tiger parents, for whom obvious academic success is the only marker of achievement.

The Rumour Monger

Closely allied to the Swan, but a much less successful player. As their child is not a high-flyer, this parent will sometimes have passive-aggressive feelings towards the parents of children who are. The Rumour Monger also tries to deflect attention from their own competitive urges by turning the spotlight on other people's alleged tiger parenting. The Rumour Monger's currency is who is being tutored and by whom, and which child is getting favourable treatment as a result of parents donating a big sum to the school library rebuilding fund. Rumour Mongers gain their status by spreading information in such a way as to create a generalised state of anxiety among other parents – and then sitting back to watch the fallout.

The Intimidator

This is the parent who will volunteer the myriad things their child is doing to get ready for an entrance exam or scholarship years in advance in order to make you back off and not even bother trying. The Intimidator will try to use the tactics of the Interrogator and the Spy to find out as much as possible about your child's levels – and then inundate you with information about their own child's achievements. This is purposely designed to send a strong message that you have come too late to the party and your child does not stand a chance. Rather than fight, you pull out – which is exactly what the Intimidator wanted all along.

The Insider

Similar to the Intimidator, these mums and dads work the system from the inside – by getting posts within key organisations vital to your child's success. Whether it's the local sports club or the school's governing board, the Insider likes to give the impression that they control access – although they often imply they have more power than they really do. The Insider knows about all opportunities, sports trials and auditions that your kids could also try for – but will never breathe a word in case your child gets picked instead of theirs.

The Assassin

Last but not least, this is the parent who lies in wait and whose self-esteem rises a notch every time they get in a dig – and you are left reeling. The Assassin knows that your child is your Achilles heel. This parent also knows that if you respond, you will look insecure and paranoid – so they trade on your paralysis. The Assassin may try to put you at your ease by complimenting your child at first – so you are caught off-guard and too confused to react when they go in for the kill. Once ambushed, you're so stunned you walk away trying to work out how they got away with it – and feeling furious with yourself for not fighting back.

REAL-LIFE EXPERIENCES

'Phoebe was eight-and-a-half months when she rolled over the first time. I was so excited that I went to my NCT group to tell the other mothers – only to find out that another baby had taken her first steps. My husband and I went to Oxbridge and assumed our baby would be the first to do everything. It was a shock.'

Annabel, first-time mother

'I used to love everything my daughter did. Then one day when she was about four she brought home a drawing with some writing on the back. At that stage she was still joining dots to make letters. But on the other side of the sheet was a full sentence in perfectly formed letters with full stops and capitals. I asked her if a child in her class had written it and when she said yes that's when the panic started and it hasn't let up since.'

Louise, mother of two

'At my son's primary, the parents have taken to communicating to teachers about reading matters via Post-it notes – or in pencil so any concerns can be removed or rubbed out. You don't want other parents knowing you have a problem when they look in the reading diaries on playdates.'

Caitlin, mother of two

WARNING SIGNS THAT YOU ARE A TIGER PARENT

- Do you use school open days as opportunities to find out how classmates' work compares with your child's? ☐

- When you see another youngster do well, is your first question to yourself: 'Why can't my son/daughter do that?' ☐

- Do you feel physically nervous before a child's exam, sports match or parents' evening? ☐

- Do you find yourself wondering about how other parents are getting their children to achieve more than yours? ☐

- Do you turn things into a competition for your children when they don't need to be, like who's cleaned their plate first? ☐

- Have you ever inflated your child's achievements to other parents? ☐

- Are you irritated when other people's children show talent? ☐

- Do you find it difficult to congratulate the parent of another child on an achievement? ☐

- Do you lack meaningful friendships with other parents? Have you worked though several relationships at the school gates? ☐

- Do you view new arrivals in your child's class as possible rivals – and try and find out what levels they have attained? ☐

- Have you developed a pattern of insisting on special treatment for your child for fear they will not otherwise get noticed? ☐

- Do you subscribe without question to theories like Malcolm Gladwell's 10,000 hour rule, which proposes that with this amount of practice, anyone can become an expert at anything, from violin to chess? ☐

- Do you find yourself racing or driving dangerously to get your children to different extra-curricular activities? ☐

There are two more subspecies of tiger parenting that are such forces in their own right, they deserve their own sections.

THE X-FACTOR/BEAUTY PAGEANT PARENT

YOU DON'T HAVE TO enter your child in one of the growing number of kiddie beauty pageants to compete on the basis of their looks. In today's X-Factor society, more parents than ever are becoming caught up in the idea that good looks are one more way to push kids to the front. Tiger parenting now gets played out in much bigger arenas than just academia, sports and the arts. Attractiveness has become one more area where competitive parents have upped the ante.

The Miss World pageant may have vanished from our TV screens, but a miniaturised version is taking place in our school playgrounds every day. Mums who married well thanks to their own good looks are often quite happy to instil in their daughters the idea that being the best-looking will get you higher up the totem pole.

For Lucy, the fact that her fifteen-year-old daughter got her tooth chipped while playing hockey came as a blessing in disguise. It gave her the excuse to get daughter Georgina's teeth veneered so she has a 'Hollywood smile'. Now Lucy has turned her attention to a competition of a different sort: seeing if her daughter will get the most requests for dates from boys at school.

Nicola likes to project the good looks of her ten-year-old daughter, Jennifer. Recently she hired a professional photographer to take some shots which she has submitted to child modelling agencies in the hopes of securing an ad campaign – something she knows will also make Jennifer the envy of her class. While they wait for their big break, Nicola thinks nothing of taking Jennifer to the hairdressers so they can both get matching blow-dries and make sure she shines at school discos. It's their way of 'doing some girly bonding'.

Parents like Nicola will also think nothing of getting their daughters' eyebrows or legs waxed, or buying them make-up while still at primary school, sending questionable messages to children that they cannot be pretty without a lot of time and effort. All this will be justified by parents by saying they are doing it for their child's confidence.

Indeed, it's tempting – not to mention fun – to turn your daughter into a mini-me – but the problem is that instead of passing on positive values and aspirations, it gives them a superficial impression of what's important in life.

Often we can lose sight of the signals we are sending out. Fears that girls will be bullied for their looks can make mothers extremely aggressive about improving their children's appearance, saying it's in their best interests to put them on diets or even, later on, pay for their plastic surgery. Even if we don't explicitly say we want children to be good-looking, we give the game away with what we notice about them, our evaluations of them, and how much time and money we encourage them to spend on their appearance.

Youngsters already compete enough over looks between themselves without parents adding to the pressure and making their appearance a big deal. In the same way as kids know where they come academically in class, I have come across girls as young as six ranking their female classmates – from one to fifteen – on a 'who's the prettiest' list.

The trend has also moved to YouTube, which has clips of primary-age pupils rating their classmates as 'hot or not' – and heartbreaking clips of girls as young as eight asking strangers to give their verdict on whether they are ugly or pretty.

By starting our children early on the catwalk of life, we short-change them – and put them on a path to endless dissatisfaction. Girls in particular start to believe that their precious time and energy should be spent on improving their looks, instead of on the things that really matter. Teachers have told me that they are infuriated by pupils spending their entire break times reapplying their lip gloss and eyeliner in the loos – and not exerting in sport because they might smudge their mascara.

Experts who go into schools to talk to children about body image are finding that boys as well as girls are prepared to spend half an hour in the mornings before school making sure their hair looks 'just right'.

While all this may seem safe – and even quite 'cute' – at primary school, by secondary school the word 'pretty' starts to mean 'sexy'. Because being beautiful is rapidly rewarded – people respond almost instantly to good looks – girls in particular start to believe that their appearance is what makes them worthwhile or special.

By competing over our children's appearance we magnify the importance of a quality that is already far too much of a deal-breaker in today's society. By all means, as parents, we must feel free to tell our children that they are attractive – otherwise they will assume they are not. But at the same time, we need to make it clear that their beauty is a small part of what they are – not *who* they are.

THE SPORTING TIGER PARENT

IT IS ON THE sports field that the true tiger parent is really unleashed. After all, as the whole point of a match is to win, parents can in this situation feel entirely justified in letting their true competitive instincts shine through.

The sidelines can also be emotional places to be. A sports pitch is nothing if not a level playing field. It's here that your child's ability – or lack of it – is demonstrated for all to see.

In an effort to keep all this at bay, at sports days parents are reminded over the tannoy that they must cheer for the whole team, not just for their own children. Some schools ban parents from the events altogether – or make sure they are kept at a safe distance.

Sporting events in particular are Eagle Dad territory. Fathers want sons to excel in the sports they love – or which they played at school. Fathers in particular cling to the belief that by pushing children harder in sports, it will make their kids tougher. The higher up the ladder a child goes – and the more visions of glory and sponsorship dance before their eyes – the more parents can lose perspective and the more destructive their coaching of their children becomes, unless they take conscious efforts to keep it in check. Never mind that even

REAL-LIFE EXPERIENCE

'It's the secrecy that gets to me. Some neighbours asked me to take their daughter once a week for a year. I was happy to oblige because she was a lovely little girl and got on well with my daughter. They didn't tell me until afterwards, but the reason they needed the childcare was so that they could take their son for lessons for a music scholarship. They didn't want to tell because they thought my son would apply too.'

Sheryl, mother of three

'One of my favourite pushy parent moments was when my three-year-old daughter took her favourite story book along to playgroup. She knew it off by heart – including when to turn the pages. I sat down next to the biggest competitive mum in the group, got the book out and suggested my little girl read it. She was word perfect. The thunderous look on the other mum's face was a classic.'

Judith, mother of two

'I don't want to dampen my friend's enjoyment of motherhood, but she seems to think it's fun to set our two kids up in competition. One minute, it's which one can sound out her letters. The next it's who can kick the ball the best. I am sure she thinks it's fun but it makes me very tense. I don't know how to address it without sounding angry and defensive.'

Kirsty, mother of one

'I first came across how contagious competitive parenting is in the park when I was pushing my son in the swing. I counted each swing up to twenty to help him learn his numbers and perhaps rather smugly waited for him to repeat them back to me. We went on the slide, but then I happened to hear the parent who had been standing next to me trying to do the same thing with his child.'

Antony, father of two

hugely talented children are continually weeded out of sports training programmes – and the likelihood of them reaching the top echelons is infinitesimally small.

Of course, the majority of us are just interested in whether our child is in the First Team, the Seconds or even selected at all. But it helps to remember that the aim of sport should be for your child to love it. Shouting – or performing a victory dance as I saw one mother do at a primary-school netball match – is counterproductive because rather than encourage a better performance, the embarrassment kids feel as a result inhibits them. Coaches observe that when pressure from parents becomes intolerable, some children feign injury during games to take the heat off themselves. Others will react by simply giving up the sport altogether.

Far from being character building, research has also found that pushing children too young into sports they are not physically ready for is bad not only for their health – it also develops feelings of inferiority. By the age of fifteen, a range of studies has found that a staggering eighty to ninety per cent of young people have dropped out of organised sport, saying it's become so competitive that it's no longer fun. By doing so they may be depriving themselves of a way to keep fit and healthy throughout their lives. So instead of asking a child after a match 'Did you win?', ask them 'Did you enjoy yourself?' Instead of victory, think of a different goal: getting your child to genuinely love sport and take part in it socially for their long-term physical and emotional health.

HOW TIGER PARENTING AFFECTS OUR RELATIONSHIPS

YOU MIGHT ASSUME THAT an issue like how much to tiger-parent children might bring up all sorts of friction in a couple's relationship. But in fact the tension between parents is rarely to do with whether they should be pushy or not. Driven, successful people tend to marry each other – and to want the same affluent lifestyle for their offspring that they enjoy. It means most couples are on the same page, reinforcing each other's aspirations, and having similar goals for their children. (One exception is sport, where dads can blindly push boys in areas they value while mums struggle to point out how their sons are hating every second.)

The real risk to a couple's relationship actually comes from the rising stress levels that build up in the home as a result of the hectic schedules that evolve when parents maximise every moment. As extra-curricular activities such as music and sport start to get more serious as children get older, they expand into the weekend. The result is that instead of spending time together, couples just end up passing the baton, ferrying children to different activities as if they were running a non-stop relay race.

This rush, rush, rush atmosphere at the very time of the week when families need to spend time together inevitably causes rows. Dianne, for example, becomes furious when her lawyer husband Tim does not quite see the urgency of getting their three children to cricket, tennis and music theory.

Dianne – who runs a small business – says: 'I'd love a lie-in too, but I don't feel I have any choice but to arrange the activities on Saturdays and Sundays. It relieves the pressure during the week, but Tim views it all as an inconvenience. He enjoys the reflected glory when the children do well, but he does not appreciate the work I put in to get them to that level. He feels he has earned the right to put his feet up at weekends. But I expect him to pitch in.'

Mums and dads may also clash over exactly what methods are needed to get a child to do well – with each partner bringing different styles and ideas of what worked from their own childhood. Grace says: 'My husband Neal comes from a family where his father, who was away a lot because he was in the army, put the fear of God into him if he didn't work hard at school – reducing him to tears if his reports weren't good enough. Neal feels that "shock and awe" tactics work – but I don't agree. I think it has precisely the opposite effect because we have a different sort of relationship with our children these days.'

Relationship counsellor and author David Code believes that parents today are too quick to put their children before their marriages – when in fact the greatest gift they can give them is the security that comes from a strong relationship. When tension starts to rise between partners, they can then start to focus even more on the children, creating a negative feedback loop. One relationship counsellor recalls seeing a couple who said they did not have time for each other because they were too busy focusing on their son, who was in a high-achieving prep school. She said: 'I asked them how it would help their son if they got divorced. For some reason, that hadn't occurred to them.'

HOW TIGER PARENTING AFFECTS OUR FRIENDSHIPS

A S ADULTS, ALTHOUGH WE may not enjoy it, we get used to dealing with competition from other grown-ups. However, we find it less acceptable when our children get dragged into the ring.

Most of us can spot a mile off the extreme parents who want to make child-rearing into a competitive sport. But with the best will in the world, in the close-knit school communities we live in, it can be difficult to completely avoid other parents who view you as a rival. And when competition creeps into established friendships or acquaintances we develop at the school gates, the result can be bitterness and simmering resentment.

First it's worth pointing out that competitive parents will only seek out other parents who have children doing well in the same areas. So if your son is scraping along the bottom of the class in numeracy, expect to be left alone by the parent who is planning to see her boy walk away with the maths prize at the end of the year.

However, if there's a parent who is heavily investing in her daughter being the best actress, and your girl gets picked for the role of Titania in 'A Midsummer Night's Dream', then you are more likely to be in the firing line. That's why other parents might genuinely be cheerfully oblivious to the fact that another member of the group is competitive – simply because their children have never presented a threat.

Note that I do mostly talk about mothers in this section. That's not to say that fathers do not compete with each other. They do. But men tend to be more certain, more blunt and more open about bigging up their kids. We are also socialised to see male competitiveness as more acceptable.

However, when hostility arises between women, it tends to get driven underground into passive-aggressive anger, which can bubble under the surface for years.

Assuming of course that you are not being competitive yourself, the reasons another parent may start gunning for you are many and varied. Some simply don't realise they are doing it. They may be too thick-skinned to realise that when they rave about their kids, you are taking it as a slight on yours. Other competitive ambushes may surprise you because they come from mothers who have so far managed to keep their insecurities well under wraps. But if your child has recently pulled ahead, it may have stung them into feeling they are not doing enough. Rather than address this directly, these mothers take it out on you with stealth attacks.

Other competitive frenemies may just be excessively ambitious; perhaps they have overcome a lot of obstacles to get where they are and were raised with a survival mentality. They may believe that a winner-takes-all attitude is responsible for their success – and apply the same principle to bringing up their children. For these women, a lot also rides on the success of their parenting – especially if they have given up a full-time career and have made the advancement of their children their mission. If their child is now their primary status symbol, they can find it very hard to entertain any competition. What it comes down to is that, in their world view, there is no room for your child and theirs to be good at the same thing.

Whatever the reasons, the bottom line is that competitive parenting damages relationships, both with real friends and playground pals, in ways which are usually irreparable. After all, the foundation of a true friendship is that you can relax and be yourself with each other. When you are constantly worried about where the next sneaky offensive is coming from, your guard is up all the time.

Of course, if you get particularly wound up by what you see as the bragging by other mothers, you may also need to examine why you are becoming so reactive. Competitive people are most annoying to other competitive people.

At first, some mothers who feel they are on the receiving end may bend over backwards not to bring out jealousy in a rival, even putting their own children down to keep the interaction on an even keel. As Anita says: 'My son is sporty. So if another mother brings up his performance in a competitive power play, I say: "Oh no, William is terrible at that." After that, they don't know what to say because you've disarmed them. Then when William outshines their son at the next match, I count on the fact they feel stupid. It's much more satisfying to let the facts speak for themselves.'

Christine describes how another mother would constantly send her links to YouTube videos showing her daughter's musical performances. 'Obviously she would do so under the guise of wanting everyone to delight in her daughter's talent, but I could tell it was more than that because she was also exaggerating her daughter's grade levels.

'The first three times, I sent back my warmest congratulations. But when my daughter really did pass her grade six in another instrument, I'm afraid I could not resist sending her back a video of a really virtuoso performance she did at a music festival. There was a long pause – a half-hearted well-done – and funnily enough I haven't heard anything back since.'

How much we are prepared to put up with depends on how much we value the friendship in the first place. Competition had never raised its head for Tricia and Mary until both their children reached secondary-school age. It changed when both their children applied for a place at the same selective state school.

'As the boys were good friends, I was really hoping they'd both get in. But after only my son got a place, my friend came round and spent the whole evening slagging off the school – spelling out in great detail what was wrong with it, how she'd never really wanted to send her child there in the first place and saying how ridiculous the entrance criteria were.

'Her child ended up going to a good school too, but my friend still never asks how my son is getting on. It's like the elephant in the room. After that I thought: "If you can't even be pleased for my child, what's the point of our friendship?" It was never quite the same after that.'

What to do

In situations like those described above, many women decided to move on and find different friendships. But if you know it's going to be difficult to avoid certain people in your close circle – or there's enough there to make you want to salvage the relationship – there are tactics you can try to keep the peace:

- If another mum makes a competitive power play, draw attention to the goals you both have in common. Remind them that while you may differ in your methods, we *all* want the best for our children.

- If you take the high road by rising above it, give the other parent what she needs and flatter her child. Keep bland conversation topics in your back pocket ready to change the subject if she keeps bragging.

- At all costs avoid using your child as a weapon to fight back because you want to 'show her'. If you up the ante, it's the children who suffer. Know when to walk away.

RETRACTING YOUR CLAWS

AFTER READING THIS BOOK, I hope you will question whether being a tiger parent is really the best way to bring up your child. But until you are ready to shed your stripes completely, here are some short-term ways to get started.

Recognise that competition sucks the joy out of parenting

If you do nothing else after reading this book, recognise this fact. Not only is there zero to be gained by comparing kids, there is so much to be lost – most of all, your appreciation of your child as a unique human being. No one in life will ever understand or love this person the way you do. So don't undermine that by being influenced by the evaluations of others.

Be honest

If you are often riled by competitive parents, it's likely you are competitive too. Ask yourself what areas you are competing over – and why you are so bothered.

Take the high road

Just because another parent is talking fondly about their child, does that really reflect on yours? Don't take it to mean that because their child is good at something, your child isn't. Maybe your friend genuinely wants to share some good news. Think of it as karma. If you support other people's kids, they are more likely to support yours. If you still think there are is a competitive move being played, distance yourself from the conversation without seeming jealous or defensive. Simply say, 'That's great.' Then move on.

Be sparing with your advice

If you have friends who are honest enough to express concern about their kids (although increasingly many won't in public), restrain yourself from rushing in with comparisons and solutions – even if you want to help. Be a sympathetic listener instead. Rebecca remembers being so worried about her son's progress that she poured out her heart to a fellow mum. 'Maybe I was making it sound more dramatic than it was because she asked me if I'd ever thought about a special school for him. Possibly she genuinely thought that would help, and meant it kindly, but as her child was going to one of the top academic schools in the area, it just came over as unbearably patronising. I couldn't bear to speak to her again.' In this highly charged climate, be warned that parenting egos are so sensitive that even well-meaning advice gets misinterpreted.

Avoid using the loud parenting voice

There is nothing wrong with being an engaged parent. But the special, smug – and usually loud – parenting voice some of us use when talking to our kids in public gives competitive parents an even worse reputation. No doubt it sounds solicitous to you. But can you deny that you've also used it to draw attention to the fact your child is doing something particularly well? Don't showboat. Whether it's your child being able to name an obscure subspecies at the zoo or knowing the difference between a papaya and a kumquat at the fruit counter, keep your encouragement of your child at a reasonable pitch. Apart from that, treating your child like a show pony sends them a dangerous message about what you value them for.

Stop rationalising

Competitive parents come up with an amazing number of ways to excuse their tiger parenting. Chief among these is 'My kids are more important to me than anything in the world', as if that makes it all OK. Question your justifications.

Separate your child from their achievements

Yes, it can be painful to see someone else's child get an accolade you think your child deserves. But it's essential to get some perspective and realise that we don't need kids to bring home certificates to get validation of our worth as parents – or them as human beings. Your child may have talents that lie outside the very narrow range of those that are traditionally recognised. Acknowledge qualities such as kindness, generosity and thoughtfulness. Aim to be the best parent by raising the best-balanced, most self-accepting child, not the most superficially successful one.

Realise that we are all in this together

Your child will never be happy or secure if you raise them with the idea that it's them against the world. Parenting is difficult enough without pitting our children against each other like little gladiators.

PART THREE

HOW TO SHED YOUR TIGER
PARENTING STRIPES

S o far this book has looked at why tiger parenting has become so pervasive and how it affects our children, their well-being and our relationships with them.

Far from making the next generation brighter, happier or more successful, I hope that the evidence I've presented shows that treating children as if they were contestants on a never-ending quiz show has the opposite effect. If they don't make it through the first round, children end up classing themselves as losers. If they do, they can become so obsessed with maintaining their status as top dog that they become child-workaholics, only to find that the prizes in the end aren't all they had hoped.

Because it's no longer OK to be average, those children who would previously have made up the vast majority in the middle ground end up giving up. Knowing they can never be perfect does not make them try harder. Realising it's not possible, they surrender. Because personal qualities – like empathy, a sense of humour, resilience – which are not measured by exam results are not valued, tragically they don't value them either.

In these pressured times, young people don't need more quizmasters than they already have. But because of the times we live in, many parents have adopted this role because they assume there's no other way to train their children to be winners.

The final part of the book will show how there are kinder, less damaging, more effective ways to help our children flourish. It will also look at how to give children the tools they need to stay strong and develop the emotional balance which is the mark of an authentically successful life.

But in order to throw off the stripes, first we need to look at the beliefs that underlie our tiger parenting instincts.

TAKE TIME TO STOP AND THINK

O UR GREAT GRANDPARENTS WOULD have been utterly amazed to see the lengths we go to to put our children at the front of the pack. Like us, they had the same primal urge to protect their children. But over the last half-century, that instinct has been blown up out of all proportion. Far from protecting, it pressurizes.

Pushy parenting has become the norm because it's so contagious. When we see other parents putting their kids forward, we feel compelled to do so too. If our kids don't get an advantage, we assume they are at a positive disadvantage. Egged on by schools dead-set on squeezing every last SATs level or A* out of their pupils, it's easy to get carried along with the tide. We get so sucked into the competition we can never stick our heads above the surface to see a way to the shore. Few of us have time to do anything but keep swimming. After all, there are bills to pay, school drop-offs to get to, extra-curriculars to sign up for…

But just for a moment, tread water and consider whether the outcome of all this effort is as certain as you thought. There is a thin line between encouraging your children and pushing them. The problem is that you often can't tell you've crossed it until it's too late. Rather than leave it until then, take the long view and ask yourself the questions you need to now.

Your relationship with your child – what do you want from it?

Imagine meeting your child in twenty years' time.

- Ask them to describe their childhood. Do they describe it as magical? Or do they look back on it as a race from one accolade to the next?

- Ask them about their relationship with you during those formative years.

- Do they say they felt loved unconditionally for who they were? Or did they pick up that the smiles and approval were more plentiful when they reflected well on you?

- Do they remember feeling less worthy of your love when they failed – or feeling afraid to face you because they feared your criticism?

Now that they are older, do you and your children have such an open, happy relationship that they want to spend time with you for its own sake? Or do they see you partly out of a sense of duty, to impress you with their latest achievements – or because they feel they 'owe' you?

What do you want for your children?

When you say you want your children to be happy, what has that come to mean to you? If you really analyse it, has it drifted into being interpreted as professional success and financial acumen? Furthermore, have you come to judge success by a very narrow definition of traditional career achievement and earning power?

Now check again. If you look around you, what do the happiest people you know have in common? Is it material goods, high-flying jobs and academic qualifications? Or is it emotional balance? If you approach the question another way, are the wealthiest people you know also the most satisfied with life?

Did your contemporaries with first-class degrees from top universities always turn out to be the most successful? Or was the equation not quite so simple? If you think about it, do you also know people who were not so-called high-flyers at school, but who did well thanks to their personal qualities and determination?

Your triggers

Next look at your tiger parenting triggers. Think about the situations in which your pulse starts to race – and where you have placed your priorities.

• Ask yourself how these feelings link back to your childhood.

• Do you value some of your child's achievements more than others because you either excelled or failed in them yourself?

• Deep down, are there qualities you want your child to have – like being more academic, thinner, prettier, more outgoing or more sporty – which are more important to you for those reasons? Has attachment to those attributes ever blurred your judgement?

WHAT YOU CAN DO

• **Value every quality:** Show your child that you value qualities other than academic success. Instead of asking what marks they got at school, ask what games they played or how their friendships are going. Recognise the fact that they have been picked as 'a playground pal' or to appear on the Good Manners board every bit as much as getting top marks in an exam. Encourage them to see themselves as well-rounded characters who are more than the sum of their achievements on paper.

• **Think outside the box:** Value careers other than white-collar professions with big salaries. It takes many different skills and aptitudes to make a world. If you only value a restrictive range of conventional jobs, like lawyer, doctor or banker, your child could end up feeling very trapped – or obliged to follow a path they have no interest in.

• **Inoculate your child:** Talk to your child about the corrosive effects of relentless competition, so they can question it for themselves. Telling them about it, rather than letting them assume it's just the way life is, allows them to decide whether to accept or reject it. It will help immunise them to the worst effects.

- **Let them be:** As their protectors, it's easy to assume we know how our children feel and what's best for them. But projecting our own memories of childhood with the benefit of hindsight stops us from empathising with the life they have now. Listen to what they are really trying to say – even if they are still struggling to find the words. Kids who think you don't understand them will give up trying to be heard.

- **Stop comparing:** The saying: 'comparisons are odious' is every bit as applicable now as it was when Shakespeare wrote it 500 years ago. There is no child in the world the same as yours. Celebrate their uniqueness. Acknowledge the combination of qualities that make them who they are. Help kids tell their own personal stories of their journey with photographs they like – and have also taken – in scrapbooks. Let them define for themselves who they are.

- **Admit your mistakes:** Parents who pretend to be faultless and hide their failings role-model unrealistic perfectionist behaviour. In turn, this encourages children to aim for impossibly high standards they can't live up to. It makes them believe they must present a perfect face to the world. Every parent makes errors, and it's not a sign of weakness. In everyday situations, parenting trainer Nadim Saad of Best of Parenting recommends the 'rewind and replay' technique if you lose control. So if you have said something to your child in anger, as soon as you have calmed down, say you'd like to replay the scene again in a more constructive, controlled way. Nadim says: 'Children appreciate honesty and they don't hold grudges.'

QUESTION THESE IDEAS

PARENTS OFTEN RATIONALISE PUSHY parenting by subscribing to some of the following beliefs. See if you recognise any of them, and check whether you are ready to question their truthfulness.

I am a success if my child is

As we have seen, this belief really took parents by the throat in the 1970s and 1980s, when they started seeing themselves as completely responsible for how their children turned out. Gradually, this sense of responsibility morphed into parents taking complete credit for their children's successes.

Children are not born to make their parents feel good about themselves. They come into the world to grow and learn within the safe environment of the family – and to become independent adults. If children come to feel like trophies, they start to feel they are valued not for who they are, but for what they do – and how good they make you look – breeding unhappiness.

I am a success, therefore my child must be

No matter how high-achieving you are, there are no guarantees that your child will arrive on the planet with the same talents and drive. Free your child from expectations about what they ought to be, based on what heritage, class or gene pool they come from. Some of the greatest damage happens when parents feel 'entitled' to a certain type of child – and get disappointed when their sons or daughters do not meet those preconceptions.

The sooner the better

In 1996, a book was published that helped change the experience of parenthood. *What to Expect in the First Year* by Heidi Murkoff was the follow-up to the global best-seller *What to Expect When You're*

Expecting (by the same author) – it is estimated that ninety-three per cent of all women who read a pregnancy book read this book.

Up until then, child development had been a relatively relaxed process for parents, who knew little about it, and generally expected stages like walking and talking to happen in their own time. As soon as the manual – and its follow-up on toddlers – was published, it became the manual for parents to see if their children were above or below the curve. Month by month, it tracked young children by three broad categories: what your baby [or toddler] will probably be able to do, what your baby may possibly be able to do, and what your baby may even be able to do. Just letting things happen was no longer enough.

Even though the books were only meant as helpful guides, they became recipes for parental neurosis, alternately helping parents puff up with pride that their tots were showing signs of giftedness – or making them lie awake at night terrified that they were lagging behind. So it was ironic when, twenty years after the first publication, the author wrote an article about becoming a grandmother for the first time in which she urged her daughter not to fret about developmental milestones for her new baby.

Complaining that society's race to attain the parenting prize had now become all-consuming, Murkoff wrote: 'Of course, there's always been competition. Put ten mothers and their babies in a room together and inevitably the comparisons will start. Whose baby is rolling already – which baby is smiling or gurgling? But back in the day, you could leave that room and those comments and comparisons behind.' Indeed.

Of course the book is now one of many to chart infant progress. But like league tables for schools, developmental milestones, oversimplified by baby books, have become a tyranny. And of course our fretting and anxiety passes, as if by osmosis, to our children – no matter how young they are.

The milestones in *What to Expect in the First Year* are based on the Denver Developmental Screening Test, developed in the 1960s to help detect serious delays early. But what was a useful diagnostic method to spot children in need of help in the hands of specialists became boiled down and obsessed over by over-involved parents, in the same way that IQ testing, which was developed in 1905 to identify children with severe delays, has also become used to pigeonhole children.

Development experts continue to tell parents that most children unfurl at their own rate – and that pushing too soon can turn children off learning. No amount of pulling a flower through the earth will make it blossom sooner. Expose a sapling to the sun too early and the stem will be weak and liable to break. Yet parents who have children reading at two still believe they are on course for Oxbridge, while those whose offspring are not reading confidently at five assume they never have a hope.

Some children genuinely do need a longer take-off – it doesn't mean they won't soar. To return to the obvious examples, Einstein didn't speak until three. Mozart may have started composing at four, but Beethoven didn't start until twelve. Both are equally great composers.

At the same time, other research shows that children who demonstrate very early skills in reading later even up with everyone else. A study published by the *International Journal of Educational Research* found that there is no difference in the literacy skills of children who start reading in nursery compared with those who start a year or two after.

Better Get Used To It

Educationalist Alfie Kohn coined the acronym BGUTI – for Better Get Used to It – to describe the current educational trend towards testing children all the time and making those tests ever harder.

The philosophy behind this is that life is competitive, and there's lots more stress and exams to come, so we'd better toughen children up as soon as possible.

However, children don't get better at dealing with hard knocks just because they get exposed to them earlier. Instead they can become test-phobic and anxious. They may brand themselves winners or losers before they've had the chance to work out their own strengths and weaknesses. They will only develop the inner strength they need to cope later if they are allowed a happy, stress-free childhood first.

It's my child versus the world

One of the most pernicious ways in which competitive parenting has made our society more brutal is that parents tend to view all children as rivals to their own. But training your kids to treat every classmate as a potential adversary can make the world a very lonely place to grow up in.

It's a cliché, but we can't afford to lose sight of the fact that it takes a village to raise a child. For one thing, most children prefer a general atmosphere of cooperation and teamwork. In party games young children will often complain that they wish everyone could win. Studies have also found that kids who are raised with a cooperative approach to their peers are likely to be more emotionally resilient, creative and open-minded, all qualities that will be needed more than ever in tomorrow's world. Furthermore, if you support and encourage other people's children, other people's children will support and encourage yours.

THE TOP TEN TRIGGERS FOR PARENTAL COMPETITION:

1 Crawling and walking milestones
2 Sleeping habits, such as whether a baby sleeps through the night
3 Reading and mathematical achievement
4 Speech development
5 Good behaviour
6 Exam results and university acceptance
7 Dancing and sporting ability
8 Breastfeeding and organic food
9 Purchase of expensive baby equipment
10 Weaning and eating habits

SOURCE: Study of 2,000 parents of children under 18 by Aviva.

HOW WE PASS ON STRESS TO OUR CHILDREN

A T THE SAME TIME as being told that we must make every moment of our child's life count, the speed of our own lives makes being a parent extremely stressful.

Modern technology and economic uncertainty combine to make working days longer. More parents than ever both work. A total of sixty-six per cent of mothers now have jobs, compared with twenty-three per cent in 1971 – often with little family support to help them juggle both roles.

At the same time the pressure on parents is stepped up due to the ever-climbing expectations that every child should excel. Increasingly schools are moving towards shifting the blame on to parents if children do not.

In working so hard to provide for our children, most of us genuinely believe we are doing the very best for our kids – and it's true that we are, in material terms at least. But we are kidding ourselves if we believe that our children are not also affected by the rising levels of angst it takes to be able to afford to buy the things we assume they need, whether it's gadgets or expensive holidays. Children in the UK have, between them, £7.3 billion worth of possessions in their bedrooms. Once a child might have owned one or two treasured soft toys or playthings. Now they are likely to own hundreds of different brands of the same type of toy.

As well as the race to get more money, there is also the race against time for parents. There is no longer just the dash to get to work. Every morning harried grown-ups can be seen sprinting behind buggies to get bewildered-looking babies and toddlers to nurseries and childminders before they can set off for work. Then the same cortisol-raising exercise is repeated in the evening when they have to peel themselves away from work and collect their offspring in time to escape late fees.

All this rushing about means that study after study finds that working parents have a dwindling amount of time with their children. After a long working day, many parents now say they are too stressed and tired even to read kids a bedtime story. Half of all British parents, who have the longest working hours in Europe, say they are forced to put their career before family life, according to The Children's Society.

Even if parents work from home – as they increasingly do in order to try and see more of their kids – their children can be more directly exposed to work stress.

Many working parents will have noticed that, according to Sod's Law, they get the most critical calls and emails towards the end of the working day as office-based colleagues clear their to-do lists. So often their timing seems to coincide with the period between pick-up and bedtime, when parents had hoped to be available for their children. Deadlines also have a habit of falling on the same days as parent–teacher evenings, or delaying pick-ups from schools – where staff are often less than sympathetic. Bosses with urgent queries rarely worry about the knock-on effects on stress levels in family homes. That's *your* problem, not theirs.

Pulled in every direction, many of today's working parents spend most of the time feeling frazzled, emotional – and sometimes unable to hold it all together. Imagine how frightening it must be for a child, who relies on his parents for everything, to see them being overwhelmed. In our rush to give our children everything, we so easily forget that anxiety is contagious and that we, the parents, set the emotional thermostat in our homes.

Animal and human studies find that when parents are stressed, their offspring are stressed too. Baby rats, for example, are more fearful and hypervigilant if their mothers are too busy to lick them and calm them down. In humans, babies who sense their mothers' anxiety feel more pain from injections, studies have found.

This symbiosis starts in the womb, when a mother's anxiety can affect a baby's development. During pregnancy, studies have found that stress can have a negative effect on IQ, immune system response and future behaviour. After birth, a study by the University of New South Wales found that anxious mums-to-be had babies who closely mirrored their stress responses.

The likely reason is that, as part of their evolution, infants come into the world with an acute sensitivity to their parents' non-verbal cues. They are so helpless that they have to learn to read their caregivers' expressions, moods and body language for their survival.

The same parent–child bond that makes a child mimic its mother's smiles cuts both ways. Just as a mother picks up on a child's distress, so the child picks up on its mother's. In other words, children can 'catch' anxiety just like they catch a cold. Like sponges, they soak up the angst that can pervade our homes until their developing nervous systems get overwhelmed. Medical studies have found that children of stressed parents get ill more often and suffer from more chronic health problems than those with more relaxed parents.

Nor does our shortage of time make the periods we do have with our children more special. One analysis of the interaction between adults and kids found that when parents try to make up for lost time, they get more bossy and intense, bombarding children with questions about what they are doing and telling them what needs to be done. Just one in four children in the UK say they talk with their mum or dad more than once a week about something that really matters.

Often when parents become overwhelmed, they are the last to see it. Fight-or-flight just becomes a way of life. There is no time to step back, so parents accept that this is what their lives have become. The truth is that placing too many demands on yourself to be the best possible parent can make you a much worse one.

Surveys have shown that what absent parents want most is to spend more time with their families – but they can't, 'because children cost so much'. We are endlessly given shock-horror figures about how much it costs to raise a child – around £100,000 from birth to age eleven at the last count – which sends us into even more of a panic. The irony is that a child might be emotionally healthier living in a smaller home or not going to a private school, rather than being cared for by two exhausted parents working round the clock to pay for a more expensive mortgage and school fees.

As a result of all this, kids take home the message that the work we are so keen to prepare them for is a treadmill. No wonder teenagers are despondent about the future when they are told they are taking exams to get the same sort of jobs that make their parents so miserable.

A study from Finland found that the stress parents feel in the workplace also affects how children do in the classroom. Researchers at the University of Jyväskylä questioned the parents in more than 500 families about whether they had ever been burnt out. It was found that the couples who were worn out physically and emotionally were more likely to have children suffering similar problems at school. The parents' negative attitudes made youngsters scared, fearful they were falling behind, and exhausted.

REACHING BREAKING POINT

ON TOP OF MONEY worries, most parents are also concerned with how their children are doing at school – almost all the time. Rather than making our children feel secure and loved, this neurotic focus makes them think there must be a lot to worry about. That's why the most over-attentive, involved parents rarely have the most confident kids.

Even so, increasingly we accept helicopter parenting – or the constant hovering over every activity – as the norm. We mistakenly believe that the more we worry, the more this proves that we are on the case. The fact that we are constantly busy still does not mean our children are left to just 'be'. Far from it. Guilt-ridden that we are letting our children down, we fuss and fret about them more in an effort to compensate. We enrol them in more extra-curricular activities to make us feel certain we are giving them every opportunity – and then have to work harder to pay for them.

Like a perfect storm, layer upon layer of stress builds up – and then we explode. Quite simply, stress overload is one of the greatest enemies of good parenting there is. It makes us forget our best parenting intentions and turns us reactive and panicky, especially when all does not go to plan.

Parents who slave around the clock to pay school fees, for example, can be more likely to become resentful and angry with their children when the dividends do not seem to be paying off. To remedy the situation – sometimes under pressure from the schools, as well – parents may then spend large sums on tutors – only to find that there is no special advantage gained because every other parent feels compelled to do the same.

The more we fret about a child's academic performance, the less able we are to deal with it rationally and calmly. In turn, the more anxious a child becomes, the less well they will do at school. Adrenalin makes every setback feel more serious and makes every reaction more knee-jerk. In our highly-strung state, anything a child does 'wrong' seems more wilful and deliberately meant to antagonise. Our parenting becomes less empathetic and more impatient. We are so busy keeping ourselves afloat that all we want is our kids to comply without question.

Without realising it, we can get angry that we seem to spend our lives in our children's service, and then even angrier they seem to always want more. Our standards slip – we become inconsistent in applying them and we opt for 'anything for a quiet life' parenting. Routines that provide safety and security go out of the window, and there are more rows about homework and bedtimes.

Feeling relentlessly put upon also creates a martyr complex, as well as a sense of raging indignation, which can allow parents to feel justified in losing control and biting the heads off both each other and their children.

Of course, we only get it back with interest. As you are their first role model, your children will learn to react the way you do. If you shout, they shout back. It doesn't take long before you hear quite young children also describing themselves as 'stressed'. Then when our kids respond to our anxiety levels by acting up, becoming tense or rebelling, we go back to the parenting books and wonder where it all went wrong.

The saddest thing is that the children from overwrought families process all this by feeling blamed. What other conclusion can they draw when they see us working around the clock on their behalf? The negativity and unhappiness can also lead them to conclude that we don't like them very much. According to Professor David Elkind: 'Young children – two to eight years – tend to perceive hurrying as a rejection, as evidence that their parents do not really care about them.' He points out that these feelings of rejection follow our children into their teens – 'the time when they pay us back for all the sins real or imagined that we committed against them when they were children'.

Counsellor David Code, author of *Kids Pick Up On Everything: How Parental Stress Is Toxic To Kids*, has spent much of his career researching how stress affects families. He wanted to get to the bottom of why affluent, well-educated people – who showered their children with love – were not necessarily getting more balanced, emotionally healthy children.

He had assumed that when kids developed behavioural problems, it was these problems which made the family tense. On closer inspection, he found it was the other way around. A family was often tense *before* the child developed an emotional issue.

Code believes that the most important message we give our children is not that we are watching and worrying about them every second of the day. It is offering them a calm, stress-free environment. It is letting them know there are no immediate threats.

Code argues that in lab experiments, when rat mothers lick their pups, the babies show lower stress levels not just because they feel cared for. Their stress levels go down because the mother is sending the message that the environment is safe enough to give her time to groom her offspring. 'A mother rat is saying to them: "Times are so good and predator- and stress-free that I have lots of time to lick you guys."'

IT'S NEVER TOO LATE

THE GOOD NEWS IS that it is never too late to adjust the emotional temperature in your home – and the effects will be instantaneous.

Putting boundaries around your work, cutting back on how much time you spend rushing kids to extra-curricular activities, taking steps to dissipate your stress build-up: all these will have an immediate effect.

Although more men are staying at home to care for children, Joan Borysenko – a Harvard-trained biologist who has studied the effects of pressure – believes women are more likely to suffer from overload because they tend to be people-pleasers who put their own needs second. For many mums, the downward spiral begins when they fall for the belief that they need to be constantly wired to get anything done. 'Women are good at multi-tasking, but when you're a working mother, there are just too many tasks,' says Joan. 'Wherever you are, you think you're in the wrong place.'

What to do

Think back to your own childhood. Recall how you felt as a child when you saw stress and anxiety in your parents' eyes, and how scared it made you feel. Keep in mind that what children want most is calm, unflappable adults.

- **Monitor yourself:** It's essential to identify what it is that tips you over the edge, says Borysenko. Simple awareness can be the best protection. 'Create a sliding scale in your head. At one end, the number one means "I'm feeling really good", and ten is "I'm feeling burnt out". Keep drawing a hatch line between those two points to work out where you stand. If it gets to an eight – and you're feeling like you can't stand it any more – it's time to take a moment to relieve the situation.'

- **Look after yourself:** There's a reason they tell you on aeroplanes to put on your own oxygen mask before helping anyone else. It's not just your child who needs sleep, good food and downtime. Take holidays as often as you can. They don't have to be expensive, but just stepping away from the daily pressures for a few days can re-establish the bond between you and your child – and put the fun back into your relationship.

- **Draw boundaries:** Bosses and colleagues will keep pushing for as long as you keep giving. They won't give a thought as to whether the stress levels in your home are being raised by emailing and ringing you out of office hours, in family time that traditionally would have been sacred. Establish boundaries by setting up auto-replies on your email and voicemail in the hours between school pick-up and bedtime.

- **Let off steam:** One of the best ways to de-stress is to simply talk to a friend in whom you can confide. If you complain to a partner, they will feel guilty and semi-responsible. They may become more stressed themselves, because they will interpret you letting off steam as a sign you can't cope, when what you really need is a pressure valve. Borysenko says: 'Partners will often try and fix your life. But we don't necessarily want that. We often just want to be able to share and confide.'

- **Cut your time drains:** While parents are good multi-taskers, sometimes there are just too many tasks. Give yourself permission to be brutal about time-sapping people or activities.

MAKING YOUR HOME INTO A REFUGE

MORE THAN EVER, YOUR home needs to be a place where your children can retreat from the world, and recharge; not simply another hothouse. Do your children love to come home after a day at school? Or do they feel they will be grilled the moment they step through the front door? Do they feel safe and able to relax – or on their guard because you are constantly on their case?

If we are always checking up on our children, pushing them to do more, they will start to look forward to seeing us about as much as we look forward to seeing a traffic warden standing over our car. Here's how to make your home a haven.

Relaxing

If your child hasn't had the best day, tell them that's fine. Life was never meant to be easy and it would be boring and unchallenging if it was. Teach children to recognise when they need to de-stress. Suggest they take a bath, come for a walk or curl up on the sofa with you and have a chat. These are small gestures. But together they give the message that home is a sanctuary.

Sleeping

Most children are sleep-deprived – and build up considerable sleep deficits during term time. This means they will not only be having trouble concentrating at school – they will be less able to control their emotions, and more irritable.

Don't back off on sleeping when children hit secondary school. Even thirteen-year-olds should be getting up to eleven hours a night. If anything, you need to be more vigilant when your child hits the teenage years. Chronic sleep problems in teens have been linked to depression, self-harm and poor exam results. Those who have not slept enough are more prone to negative emotions such as fear, anger and poor behaviour.

If your child is doing their homework late into the night because they got down to it late, don't start compromising on bedtimes – or they could soon be burning the midnight oil so often they become impossible to live with. Instead help them get organised. Help kids get into the habit of pacing themselves; get them to tackle the most difficult subjects first and train them to complete homework within the allotted time – with a timer if necessary, so it does not extend endlessly into the evening. (See the section on homework later in the book.)

Eating together

Family mealtimes are increasingly fragmented as a result of different timetables, extra-curricular activities and parents working longer days. A survey of British households found that fourteen per cent of families never eat together – because of the triple whammy of technology, TV viewing and the long-hours culture – both for adults and children.

Simply eating together on a regular basis not only bonds parents and children, though. It is also one of the single biggest predictors of success for youngsters. Children who eat four meals a week with their families have been shown to score higher in academic tests, and girls in particular have also been found to have higher levels of self-esteem. Other studies have found that children who eat with their parents have fewer conflicts during adolescence and are better adjusted in general. One recent study published in the *Journal of Adolescent Health* found that family meals have a calming effect – and every meal young people have with their family leads to an improvement. It found they feel more included and valued, even if they do not say much at the table, because they are able to see the communication between other members of the family and feel that they are an important part of the unit.

It does not have to be just dinner. Weekend brunches or breakfasts will work just as well too. Make the rules only that you will turn off the TV, put away your phones (try introducing a basket into which all go automatically before the meal starts) and steer clear of parental pep talks.

Make kids stronger and more able to cope by feeding them healthy, balanced meals, free from additives and unhealthy types of fats and sugar. It's said so often that it's become a cliché, but sending children off with a good breakfast of slow-release carbs and protein really does set them up for the day.

As children move into the teenage years – and parents tend to leave them more to their own devices – it's easy to leave what they eat up to them. But given the choice, most teens will opt for junk food when out and about, which can play havoc with blood-sugar levels. A young person who is on a roller-coaster of hunger followed by quick-fix sugar hits will be less able to regulate their moods and concentrate. Regular family mealtimes are a way to give your child the balanced mix of nutrients they need.

Exercising

British children spend disproportionately large amounts of time in front of screens, compared with those in other Western European countries, according to studies by Public Health England. Research has found that excessive screen time (more than four hours a day) was linked to anxiety and depression and was responsible for limiting a child's opportunity for social interaction – and of course getting them outside to get exercise. The more time they spend in front of a screen, the worse their behaviour becomes.

Something as simple as getting children outdoors makes them

immediately less stressed and allows them to feel better about themselves. One study from the University of Essex shows that 'green' exercise in the open in particular can boost mood, physical fitness and self-esteem. When measuring the effect on well-being, it's interesting that how long you spend on the exercise does not seem to make a difference. A 30-minute walk round does as much good for the state of the mind as a long trek in the countryside.

Finally, exercise can also improve children's memory. A study by the University of Illinois found that the fittest children tend to perform better on tests of their recall. The more difficult the subject matter, the better they did compared with unfit kids.

Think about getting a pet

Pets can teach children an incredible amount about responsibility and unconditional love. They also get children out of the house, reduce cortisol levels and release feel-good endorphins. In one study, children aged between nine and sixteen were asked to read aloud from a book – once with a friendly dog next to them, and then again without. It was found that the children's blood pressure and pulse rate were lower when the dog was present.

HOW TIGER PARENTING TURNS CHILDREN INTO THEIR OWN WORST ENEMIES

'Children need models more than they need critics.'
Joseph Joubert, philosopher

LOLA SITS BACK IN the therapist's chair and pinpoints the evil culprit responsible for making her believe she is stupid. The ten-year-old paints a picture of a nasty woman with a mean face and beady eyes who stands over her impatiently.

But the person who has made Lola panic whenever she has to take a test is not a teacher. It's the self-critical voices coming from inside her own head. When the therapist asks her who is talking, Lola replies quietly: 'It's me – but the mean me.' When asked to draw the person, Lola depicts an angry, disapproving figure with hands on hips and a grimacing mouth open in carping criticism, spouting the words: 'Blah, blah, blah.'

Just a generation ago, it was not unheard of for a parent or teacher to think that it was acceptable to tell a child they were hopeless at a subject, would never be good at sport or music – or would never amount to anything. This was an era in which it was still believed that shaming children worked as a way to guide them towards the right behaviour or make them work harder. It's an approach which, thanks to a better understanding of children's minds, we have since discarded because we know how much long-term damage it causes.

However, that's not to say that today's children don't feel very criticised in many other ways. These days our over-involvement with our offspring means we engage in criticism in another form – the constructive kind. Just because the bluntness of the words has been softened – or phrased differently – does not mean they have any less impact. They just come in a different style and form.

Now we have assumed the role of our children's trainers, we feel entitled to continually bombard them with suggestions about what they should be doing better. While well-dones get showered on our children so much they no longer mean anything, our missiles of criticism tend to be a lot more carefully guided. Gradually, without us even realising it, children can feel damned much more than praised. Naturally parents think they are simply pointing out where kids are going wrong so they will get it right next time. After all, our motives are good. It's well-meaning encouragement – isn't it? Some parents fool themselves that they can sneak in criticism under the radar like this – but children still get the message loud and clear.

Furthermore, even if a child's done well, many of today's parents in this ambitious atmosphere are still never satisfied. I remember seeing a father clap to his daughter enthusiastically from the side of a swimming pool. No sooner had the five-year-old let go of the side and made her first tentative strokes on her own without armbands, than he said: 'Now try swimming a width.' No doubt he felt he was being a great father by pushing – and also being seen to do so by the other parents nearby – her into achieving more. All she heard was 'nothing I ever do is good enough'.

After all, it's not what we say that matters. It's what our children actually hear. While some more thick-skinned children will learn to filter out these messages, other more sensitive ones, and especially those with negative dispositions, will internalise the voices and begin to talk to themselves the same way. This criticism starts earlier than ever for children today. Our expectations of what kids should be able to do at a very young age have become higher. We are so obsessed with the idea that sooner is better that our correction of them starts earlier too. By starting so early, we raise them as approval junkies, whose self-worth depends on our opinion.

This criticism also starts earlier for children today. Our expectations of what kids should be able to do at a very young age have become higher. We are so obsessed that sooner is better, that our correction of them starts earlier.

Children are still toddlers when they start picking up on our judgements, because we are constantly rating them – and often subconsciously ranking them alongside others of the same age.

Furthermore, our scrutiny of every brush stroke, ball catch or note they sing or play means that in an effort to 'improve' our children, criticism rains down on them almost continually.

Even if parents do not verbalise it, children pick up on the fact that not even the most innocent of pursuits – like drawing a picture or singing a song – is done for the love for it. Everything they do is assessed as an achievement.

Despite all this, today's children have little resilience to allow them to cope with the expectations heaped on them. We have taken away the tools that in past generations would have protected them by enabling them to preserve their sense of self. Kids are not given the time to work out who they are because they are never left alone long enough to think for themselves or to discover their independence. Because they know no other truth, they don't have the ability to question our views.

As we are the most important and powerful people in their lives – the ones whose opinions are supposed to matter the most – children tend to believe that if we say things, they simply must be true.

And this is perhaps why criticism has been found to be the single most important factor in a child's perception of their relationship with their parent, even into adulthood.

What to do

Mind your language

Many parents resort to 'shock and awe' tactics to show their children they mean business. When we worry so much about our children's performance, often it doesn't take much for one thought to trigger an explosion of stress – which results in us yelling at our children. Say your child's last Spanish test was a disaster, but they have now announced – the night before their next one – that they have not brought home their book to revise. In this case, your brain is swirling with anxiety. Spanish used to be their strong point. They need to stay in the top stream to feel good about themselves. What will their teacher think? How could they not care?

At times like these, our 'reptile brain' – the basic instincts of fight-or-flight that kick in before our higher thought processes have had a chance to modify them – takes over. It's in these moments that we end up saying things we regret to our children. These can make the factors that led up to your child not bringing home their books in the first place (fear of failure, avoidance) even worse.

Shouting may make you feel better in the short term. For a fleeting moment, it gives parents the illusion that we are in control. As anxiety levels rise among parents, outbursts become more likely. We may feel we are jolting our children into action with home truths, and that once the floodgates have opened, we might as well get it all out there in the open. But such wholesale attacks can be devastating for children.

It's these 'While I'm at it…here's another thing' explosions that can cause long-lasting hurt, because they tend to include universals such as 'You never bring your books home' and 'You never revise for tests' –

making a child feel they are branded for life and there's no hope of change.

If you are tempted to keep going, just don't. Shaming children into action does not work. They may be too proud to tell you that they already judge themselves pretty harshly. Turning the volume up on your criticism will just confirm that whatever negative, self-critical voices they hear in their heads are true. They are likely to feel bad about themselves as it is, without you turning on the guilt. Shouting at a stressed child has been found to cause long-term damage that is worse than smacking. One of the simplest ways to reduce levels of stress in your children is to speak to them politely, tell them you are on their side and work out how to fix a problem together.

Let your praise stand on its own

As far as possible, let your praise go unqualified if your child has done something well. If you stick to more positive feedback, your child will spend less time defending themselves and be more open to what you have to say when you do have a suggestion. According to happiness coach Shawn Achor, ensuring a ratio of five positive interactions to every negative one is the best way to help your child feel confident and flourish.

Teach them to evaluate opinions

Children tend to believe that just because something has been said about them, it must be true. Sensitive or quiet children in particular, who believe it's rude to disagree, may just accept these opinions as fact and internalise them. Show children the difference between a point of view and a fact. Train them to ask for the evidence and question who is saying what, and why. Though opinions from people with experience and who have their best interests at heart may be useful and help them appraise their own performance, other views from less well-intentioned or less qualified people, including classmates, relatives or biased teachers, may be less so. Help children spot the difference. If your child asks your opinion about a piece of work, ask them what they think first. It's their assessment which matters most.

Practise self-control

Good parenting is as much about what you *don't* say as what you do say. The challenge is to control your own outbursts and anxieties – and not pass them on to your children – and stick to words that help, not hinder. Stop the relentless performance reviews you imagine are keeping your child sharp and competitive. Even with the best intentions, the likelihood is that they are not. Imagine how you'd feel if your boss came home with you every night. If you are so exasperated with your child's performance that you feel about to burst into a volley of criticism, first ask yourself these questions:

- Am I really saying this for the benefit of my child, or because it will make me feel better?
- Am I assuming that by shouting I will shock or shame my child into doing better?
- Am I telling my child something they already know? Is my child likely to be well aware of this already?
- Am I asking for something that is developmentally appropriate for their age?
- Would this be better coming from a teacher who can be more objective?
- If I still feel this would really help, could I find a less fraught, less confrontational time when my child is more likely to take the message on board?
- Can I also say something constructive?

Instead of criticising, encourage self-assessment. It's what your child thinks of what they have done that should matter the most. Ask them what they think before stepping in with your opinion.

Help them to help themselves

When it comes to academic subjects, if a child is anxious, shouting at them about their failure to organise themselves or tackle it will be counterproductive, because this will increase the anxiety around it.

Instead train children with the skills they need to organise themselves.

This is not tiger parenting. This is simply showing them how to cope. Schools expect so much these days – but has your child ever actually been shown how to take notes, revise or fill in her homework diary with the detail it needs? Surprisingly, the likely answer is 'no'. For example, show kids how to make a Mind Map, which will help them organise their thoughts visually and remember things better.

We expect children to pack so much into their schedules, yet we rarely show them how to prioritise – an absolutely crucial skill to help them stay organised and in control. While you shouldn't do their homework for them, you can teach them how to avoid procrastination, delay gratification and cope calmly if they don't understand an assignment, so they can help themselves – and so win back more time.

HOW TO TACKLE NEGATIVE SELF-TALK

TAKE NOTE IF YOUR child is starting to do themselves down. If a child says they're stupid, a good mark wasn't deserved or often says other children are always doing better than them, these are clues that they are starting to think negatively about themselves.

Even when they do well, children with low self-esteem will dwell on the higher scores of peers in order to support their poor view of their own abilities, in a self-perpetuating downward spiral. Look out for the signs of this happening so you can help your child start to think positively again.

- **Affirm the qualities they do have:** Criticism doesn't make children try harder. It makes them give up trying. Acknowledge the talents a child has so they feel better about themselves and are more open to learning.

- **Tell kids it's not possible to be perfect:** It's not fair, or loving, to expect your child to be perfect. Nor is it fair for children to expect perfection of themselves. 'Ask children to have a look at what perfect means,' says neurolinguistic programming practitioner

Jenny Foster. 'Tell them if they were 100 per cent perfect in everything, there would be no room to improve, and point out how boring would that be.' By being given permission to scrap unrealistic targets, children stop seeing themselves as falling short and are kinder to themselves.

- **Challenge 'never and always' thinking:** When your child says they *always* get a bad mark, or will *never* be good at sport, challenge their statement and put it back into perspective. It's not enough to say: 'That's not true.' Children need to be retrained to think differently. Challenge them to be more realistic in their appraisal of themselves and adjust their thinking to help shrink their problems back to their real size. Tell them that just because they failed today, it doesn't mean they always will.

- **Start listening:** When a child has even a slight concern, parents often panic and feel the need to 'fix' it – or even impose a solution. Instead hear them out, reflect back what they are saying to show you have truly understood – and ask them to talk through the possible options. The likelihood is that they will come up with the most practical, realistic solutions themselves.

- **Get help:** If your child is stuck with negative thought patterns, getting help is not a sign of failure. The reason your child is thinking like this may be down to a complex cocktail of causes – the competitive atmosphere in schools, having too much to live up to at home and a glass-half-empty temperament can all contribute. It may take an expert to help them identify the negative voices – and teach them they do not have to listen to them. It's particularly important to address such thinking quickly in competitive school environments, where negative-thinking children can rapidly get sucked into the quicksand.

GIVING THE RIGHT SORT OF PRAISE

A T THE OTHER END of the spectrum from carping criticism is knee-jerk empty over-praising that undermines confidence, rather than improves it.

Many tiger parents believe they are bolstering their children by constantly telling them how 'amazing' they are, for everything from getting dressed in the morning to eating their dinner.

You may feel good about it, believing it gives you parenting brownie points. But the problem is that after a while your child has heard 'Well done' so many times that it has become meaningless, so it's like water off a duck's back. Many parents also make the mistake of thinking that praising their children gives them a free pass to criticise all the time, too.

For sensitive children in particular, reeled-off compliments don't permeate – but unfortunately the criticism does. As children get older and go out into the real world, they soon cotton on to the fact that not everything they do is 'fabulous' – and that you're just saying that because they are your child. They stop believing your assessment – and their faith in your judgement is diminished.

Furthermore, bigging your child up more than is deserved can actually end up short-circuiting self-esteem. If your child takes this on board, the danger is that they will build their self-image on a fantasy of superiority that will inevitably be toppled by reality. Too much praise can also send the damaging message to the child that the parents are claiming credit for their achievements.

If you have a more modest, introverted child, public cheerleading may also have the opposite effect from that intended. No matter how proud you are, a relatively shy youngster may become embarrassed or reluctant to accept compliments, even when they are due, because they dislike all the fuss and feel they are not justified, particularly in the context of today's harsh school environment

It can also send the damaging message to the child that the parents are claiming credit for their achievements.

Stanford psychology professor Carole Dweck has also found

that parents praising children for qualities such as being clever can seriously backfire and damage children's motivation. When children hear they are brilliant, or hugely talented, they interpret this to mean that they are lucky enough to have been bestowed a genetic gift over which they have no control. Dweck also found that children who were told they were intelligent didn't bother to keep trying, because they either thought they already had what it takes – or else did not want to disprove the very lofty assessment of them.

In one experiment, a group of children was asked to solve a set of maths problems. After the first set of questions, one group was told 'You did really well. You're so clever.' The other was told: 'You did really well. You must have tried really hard.' Next, both groups were given a more difficult set of problems. Those who had been told they were clever did worse. Those who were praised for trying fared better because they were not as worried about getting the answer wrong.

Dweck says it's crucially important for parents to instil 'a growth mind-set' in which children are praised for the qualities they have control over, like persistence and effort. Instead of telling children they have permanent traits that parents are judging, a growth mind-set tells children they are constantly evolving and are able to improve. Dweck says: 'Does this mean we can't praise our children enthusiastically when they do something great? Should we try to restrain our admiration for their successes? Not at all. It just means that we should keep away from a certain kind of praise – praise that judges their intelligence or talent. Or praise that implies we're proud of them for their intelligence or talent rather than the work they put in.'

What to do

- **Don't put others down:** Against our better judgement, it can be tempting for parents to think they're boosting their child's esteem by coming out with things like 'I bet you're the best at football' or 'You're the prettiest girl in your class'. But this kind of one-upmanship not only encourages children to repeat this kind of sentiment – making them unpopular with their peers – it also teaches them that they are only valued by how well they do compared with others. Instead let their achievements stand in their own right.

• **Don't overdo the cheerleading:** As much as you may want to show off your child's talents to the world, be aware that you risk making your child self-conscious. You may think you are being encouraging (and showcasing what a good parent you are into the bargain) by plastering every scribble they do on the fridge – or posting their performance on Facebook – but let them decide what they want to share. Imagine if every tiny thing you did was filmed for posterity and made a fuss of. An innately modest youngster will feel much more comfortable with specific, low-key words of acknowledgement.

SIGNS THAT YOUR CHILD COULD BE FEELING STRESS

The crucial difference between adults and children is that children can recognise or understand why they feel they way they do, let alone know what to do about it.

How a child responds to an overly pressurised environment will vary according to many factors: their temperament, their genetic make-up, their resilience, their success at school, their personal stress threshold and also their relationship with their family.

If they do start to feel affected, at first it can be hard for parents to tell the difference between what is a normal stage of childhood, and what might require some help – especially as research has found that children who show signs of anxiety in primary school are more likely to develop full-blown stress in adolescence.

Some of the early signs in young children may include:

• Saying they just want to go home and play.
• Using a whispering voice in class.
• Saying they don't deserve good marks – or pointing out how much better other children are doing, and ripping up work.
• Asking to go to the toilet a lot in lessons.

- **Tell them to compete for their personal best:** Tell children there is only one person in life who is truly worth beating; themselves. Best of all, with perseverance and practice, a child will usually win. Parent educator Noël Janis-Norton says: 'Teach children to compete with themselves – and cooperate with others. That way children can feel a sense of achievement and improvement – without having to put someone else down.' Take time to go through your child's exercise books to show how their handwriting has gone from messy scrawls to well-formed cursive, scribbles have morphed into carefully crafted drawings or their first tentative notes on an instrument have turned into polished pieces. If they are shown how far they have come by themselves, they will also see how far they can go.

Avoiding eye contact when talking to a parent.

Stopping enjoying activities they used to enjoy.

Fidgeting, hair-twirling, chronic nail-biting and skin-picking.

Showing a lower tolerance to frustration than normal; shouting without making much sense or flying off the handle.

Having a sad look and difficulty smiling, which may be remarked on by others in the family or at school.

Starting to express feelings of helplessness, hopelessness and worthlessness.

Experiencing chronic worry, becoming overly panicked by small things and thinking small setbacks are the end of the world.

Having trouble sleeping.

Finding excuses not to go to school.

Talking less and less.

Suffering unexplained stomach pains and tension headaches.

Suffering physical symptoms such as mouth ulcers, cold sores, eczema or panic or asthma attacks.

Showing OCD-like symptoms such as frequent washing of hands, arranging possessions or developing rituals that they insist on doing.

WHY WE HAVE TO STAY CONNECTED

REMEMBER THE STORY OF BELLA – AND HOW SHE AND HER PARENTS GREW APART?

WHEN CHILDREN ARE BEING fast-tracked through the education system, time with them can be at a premium. If, in the time you do have together, they come to feel constantly judged, they may stop opening up. Hurt by criticism, they may decide they have no choice but to protect their egos – and retreat into their shells. Because they feel rejected, they will in turn reject you.

For this reason it's even more important that we work on keeping a close bond; a connection that is going to be absolutely essential when the going gets really tough in the teen years. Children can feel reduced to academic automata at school – so you can see how important it is for parents to find time to be with them away from the daily grind of schoolwork and to appreciate them as individuals. If your child has withdrawn from you, you may need to make a concerted effort to bring them back – and help them learn to trust you again.

Psychologist Oliver James recommends a technique called Love Bombing. This involves spending a period of time alone with your child, offering them unlimited love and control in order to re-establish the trust between you. James also believes that taking your relationship back to its roots (perhaps before the competitive pressures started to push you apart) can stabilise the levels of the fight–flight hormone cortisol, which may be keeping your child in a constant state of apprehension.

If your relationship has been damaged by failure and criticism, it won't recover overnight. You will see improvements fast, but it can be a year or two before your child completely returns. Be patient.

However, don't wait until your relationship with your child has broken down. Set aside special one-on-one time to invest in it. Find slots when it's just the two of you – when you can just 'be' together – with no strings attached and no teachable moments. Go for a walk in the park or a hot chocolate, so your child has the chance to say things they otherwise would not have the opportunity to say.

What to do

- **Teach optimism:** Psychologist Martin Seligman's research has found how childhood optimism offers powerful protection against depression and anxiety in later life. Even if your child naturally has a glass-half-empty disposition, positive thinking can be learnt at any age. One study found that something as simple as asking children to practise thinking of three things a day they are grateful for dramatically increases how good they feel about the future.

- **Don't say never mind:** In an effort to encourage our children to do well, tiger parents can end up telling their kids how they *should* feel – in other words how we would *like* them to feel. The result is that children start to feel that their anxieties are inconvenient to us. If your child expresses worries about testing or academic subjects – or anything else for that matter – don't say 'Never mind' or 'It doesn't matter'. One of the reasons young people may self-injure, for example, is that their emotions are dismissed as wrong. Self-harming becomes a child's way of expressing what is not allowed. So acknowledge your child's feelings – and assume they are real – however trivial you consider the reasons behind them. Trying to bully children out of their worries drives them underground, and they may resurface later in much more dangerous ways. Talking to children about how they feel shows them that you are their ally.

- **Teach children to know themselves:** In the same way that children can be taught to read, they can be taught to identify and handle their feelings. When children don't know how they feel, they don't know how to make themselves better. Psychologist Daniel Goleman put forward the idea that children can also be taught to be self-aware and to regulate emotions, which has been found to be more important than IQ because it helps children make better choices about how to apply themselves and avoid risky behaviour. Start by explaining to children how you feel, how you take responsibility for your emotions and how you deal with them. As they grow, show children how to recognise, express and deal with their own feelings.

- **Keep physical contact:** As they get older, we tend to hug our children less. It is easier to put your arms around a cute toddler in your lap than a stroppy teenager who is as big as you. Scientists have found that hugging for just twenty seconds is enough to boost levels of the feel-good hormone oxytocin and keep them up the whole day. As teens become more self-conscious, find other ways to show reassurance and affection physically, even if it's just with a squeeze of the hand or a stroke of the back.

- **Lighten up:** As the pressure mounts in academic subjects, it's easy for the fun to go out of your relationship and to constantly look worried around your children. They will interpret this as meaning that there is a lot to be anxious about and that you are never pleased with them. Lighten up and take active steps not to let the tension mount. Develop in-jokes to keep you close; watch silly videos together. Add silly emoticons to your texts so not every message is a nag.

- **Reveal the bigger picture:** Ask them to find out the answer to questions like 'Why am I here?' and 'Who made the universe?' so that your child considers their place in the world – beyond exam results. For a start, show them Carl Sagan's short film *The Pale Blue Dot* on YouTube which – in the space of three minutes – manages to put human life in perspective.

- **Keep talking:** During times of conflict, your teenager in particular may appear to tune out much of what you have to say. Don't be discouraged. Just because they adopt a mask of indifference does not mean they don't care. Even if your child acts like they are not listening, choose your words wisely but keep talking. Listen and repeat back what your child is saying so that she understands that you have heard and understood. If they are scared or panicked about their exam results, for example, try to find out what they think is the worst-case scenario – and how they could survive it.

THE HOMEWORK BATTLE

Homework has a tendency to turn your home into a war zone – with you as the drill sergeant. It is one of the most common flashpoints – the crossroads at which academic endeavours meet parental expectations at close quarters – and behind closed doors.

Homework is the time when parents, exasperated that the task is not being done quickly enough, or to their satisfaction, are most likely to erupt. It is at these moments that tiger parents are most likely to blurt out things they regret in an effort to make a child perform.

Surveys have found that homework is the single biggest source of friction between children and parents. One survey found that forty per cent of kids say they have cried during rows over it. Even that figure seems like an underestimate.

The rising conflict is partly due to the fact that schools are now more likely to set formal written homework at a younger age, according to Professor Sue Hallam of the Institute of Education at the University of London. 'In the past children would be sent home with a spelling list of ten words and be expected to learn their times tables,' says Professor Hallam. 'What is happening now is that children (of the same age) are given written work, and that's where the problem starts. Mum and dad try to help and of course teaching methods have changed and that can confuse them. Parents get upset and the child gets upset.'

Yet more and more, it is being recognised that homework undermines family time and eats into hours that should be spent on play or leisure. A straightforward piece of work that would take a child twenty minutes at school can easily take four times as long at home with all the distractions and delaying tactics that go with it.

As a result, children get less sleep, go to bed later and feel more stressed. Even the weight of the books is taking its toll. A generation ago, kids would have brought home a couple of books in a satchel. Even though much homework is now set over the internet, children often carry around so many books that they develop back problems. A survey of 1,200 children by the British Chiropractic Association found that more than seven out of ten have suffered pain from carrying heavy bags to and from school.

Homework is even starting to take over the summer holidays. Once the long break was seen as a chance for children to have adventures, discover themselves and explore nature. Now the summer months are viewed as an extension of the academic year – a chance for kids to catch up…or get ahead. One in four parents now hires a tutor during the summer holidays, lest their children lose ground.

Yet, although children can slide over the holidays if they don't keep their skills up, research is showing that heavy term-time workloads do not improve performance. Finnish children, who do less homework than the British, score considerably better in international tests – coming close to the top of the table for maths and science at all ages. In France the government has proposed an end to homework in primary schools, saying that independent learning should take place at the end of the day on school grounds. Meanwhile Denmark has tried 'homework-free' schools, resulting in fewer pupils dropping out and better grades.

Homework also abides by the law of diminishing returns. Researchers at Duke University found that after a maximum of two hours of homework, any learning benefits rapidly start to drop off for secondary-school pupils.

So what are your options? You could choose a school that has decided to set less homework. One such example is Tiffin Boys in Kingston-upon-Thames, Surrey, one of the best performing schools in the country. Here teachers decided to scale back homework because of fears that it was leaving pupils depressed.

Yet at the same time, some tiger parents will ask for more, especially in primary school. If asked, teachers will go along with setting extension tasks in an effort to prove that they are giving pupils a rigorous education, even though by the time they are midway through secondary school, children can be doing four hours a night on top of a full school day.

While some children will do everything to avoid doing it, at the other extreme some will become perfectionists who have to be persuaded to go to bed. Some mothers I spoke to had to bribe their children to do less. But beware of basking in the glow of their natural conscientiousness. You may feel smug when your eight-year-old writes a three-page story, instead of the eight paragraphs the teacher was expecting. But in secondary school, these are the children who end up working away past midnight, and who later turn into students too worried to hand in their doctorates. For most children homework remains a fact of life. So your best bet is to get into a routine to ringfence it so it becomes as painless as possible. Shift your perception of what it means. Homework is not an opportunity for your child to make up for failing to excel at school, or the chance to bring honour to the family name, with you collaborating with them on such an outstanding piece of work that all competitors are vanquished. Face up to the fact that your involvement, however brilliant, isn't fooling anyone and will not instantly raise your child to the top of the class. For you and your child's sanity and relationship, treat homework simply as a job that has to be done as efficiently as possible.

What to do

To reduce conflict, train your children in good habits and place time limits on how long homework should take from the start. In today's school environment, you will be actually reducing the pressure on your children if you set up timetables and good study practices which train them to work more efficiently.

Noël Janis-Norton, author of the essential handbook *Calmer, Easier, Happier Homework*, recommends asking the school how long a child should spend on each subject at night. Then you can help keep those limits in place by telling kids they can't spend a minute more – or a minute less – than the allotted time.

Find the time of the day after school that works best for your child – either straight after arriving home or after a short break. Agree a start time every day so that the rule turns into a routine and there is less room for resistance and negotiation.

Noël says: 'That makes it clear from the start how much time is available. Within a day or two, they will start completing it in the period allowed.'

To make sure it's done to its optimum standard, but without doing it for them, Noël suggests a think-through: five minutes where you ask your child questions about what they need to do to do a good job. Refresh your child's memory by asking them questions like 'Do you need to write full sentences?' or ' Do you have to show your working?'

However, don't get too involved. Hovering over them will give them the impression they can't do it by themselves. Don't finish their homework for them because you are desperate to get it off the evening's to-do list. That will just mask the problem and get you dragged into a nightly conflict.

Of course, there is the still the possibility that the work really is too hard for them, or that they have missed a step and don't understand. If so, check with their teacher. 'Remember, the job of the teachers is to teach,' says Noël. 'The job of the parent is to teach good habits. Children are only learning when it's their brain that's coming up with the answers.'

Now you have helped children make more time, it's important that it's not just poured into computers, TV and videogames. Noël says: 'One way to prevent this is to keep all screens in areas of the house that you can easily supervise. If they break this rule, confiscate the computer for a few days, even if it means they are marked down.'

And finally, set a rule that homework must be done before they can get fun screen time – so leisure and schoolwork don't get mixed.

EXTRA-CURRICULAR ACTIVITIES

ONCE, WHEN CHILDREN CAME home, the main job of the day was done. They'd have a snack and go out to play. Homework was so minimal and the pressures so much less that most parents didn't worry that kids weren't being 'kept busy'.

They didn't have to worry about where their children were going on the internet, and felt comfortable leaving them to play in the garden – even in the street – or in front of the TV watching safe, age-appropriate programmes like Vision On or Bagpuss.

In those days there were still hobbies too: quaint ideas like stamp collecting. But that fell out of fashion due perhaps to the fact that there's no obvious high-flying career in philately.

For today's children, the sounding of the school bell at the end of the day is just the start of the second shift. New classes arrive on the market every day, starting younger and younger. Once parents were content to leave swimming, gym and sport to schools. Now flick through the back pages of any parenting magazine and you will find that if there's a talent that will look good on a CV, there's a mini-me version of it starting sooner than ever. As with the educational toy companies, businesses have been very quick to cash in on parents' fears that they can never do enough for their children, convincing them that some of the things that kids would do naturally – if they were given the time and the space – should be taught by professionals. Near me, for example, there are den-building lessons for kids, even though an afternoon left to their own devices in the woods would work just as well.

As 'professional' parents, we positively itch to enrol our daughters and sons in foreign-language classes as soon as they can gurgle, telling ourselves they will be better suited to the global job market in years to come. And we fork out a small fortune in the process. Being seen as willing to go the extra mile – and pay for more activities – has become the badge of our commitment as a parent. There are few of us who haven't signed up to something because we've heard another parent has – and because we experience FOMO – fear of missing out.

Paying someone else to give our children extra-curricular activities is also a way to feel better about being away from our children. It's feel-good, intensive, goal-orientated childcare at its most expensive.

There are of course benefits. Getting kids successfully involved in sport, for example, has been associated with higher levels of self-confidence and academic performance, more involvement with school, fewer behaviour problems and lower likelihood of drug-taking and risky sexual behaviour. But if activity attendance is allowed to become scattergun, there is a price to pay. Our stress levels rise as we become social secretaries, juggling complex schedules worthy of a CEO and paying ever-higher fees – and all this before they've even started their homework.

We call in 'experts' to teach them (though in truth many are anything but), when most of the time we could be encouraging children to do many of the things on offer on their own. We send children on expensive courses, when they would learn more about life and feel more competent if they were trained to do a few chores around the house. Do they really need cooking lessons when it would be far less time-consuming (not to mention more convivial and cheaper) to let them learn alongside you at home? The irony of all this is that our kids are more likely to know how to fence than to unload the dishwasher or set the table. Yet so often we don't value what comes for free.

We also tend to keep children in activities far too long. Children may like a class at first. But as soon as they show even the slightest sign of being good at something, we flog it to death, killing off any inner motivation they had to do it in the first place.

A recent study found that the result of all this is that over-anxious parents are making children 'work' for more than fifty-four hours a week – more than the average adult spends in the office – even though it's essential that children also have downtime to process what they are learning.

According to another piece of research, it's not about the amount of time children spend in extra-curricular activities – it's about the pressure they feel under as a result. What stops making it fun are the goals parents start attaching to the activities, says Suniya Luthar, a psychology professor at Columbia University's Teachers College.

Andrée Aelion Brooks was one of the first to call attention to the over-scheduled child. For her book *Children of Fast-Track Parents* she interviewed eighty mental health professionals and educators, in addition to sixty parents and around a hundred children. Brooks found that putting kids into extra-curricular activities is not always a good idea. With too many commitments and responsibilities, she found that some kids can develop stress disorders.

Take that trip twenty years into the future again. Do you think your children will remember the dizzying array of activities they were signed up for? Or will they remember how tired they were and you telling them off for not being ready on time for the next extra-curricular class?

Of course, you may well have helped them discover a special talent.

But if they are still enjoying that talent in twenty years' time, it will be because they poured their heart into it, not you.

What to do

- **Give them downtime:** Kids need downtime to process and take in what they are learning. Children's cognitive performance increases when they spend less time in regimented whole-group activities and more time in free play, according to research.

- **Don't start too young:** Mostly young children need their parents – and will learn more from fun interaction with you than from an organised music class or baby gym sessions. Doing too much, surrounded by too many children, can make babies and toddlers clingy and insecure. For them a trip to the park is just as exciting. Ask yourself too if you are creating a busy timetable because you are not sure what to do with them at home. Make sure any groups you do join are not too large and are manageable for young children.

- **Check your motives:** Have you signed up your child to an activity because they really like it – or because you think it's giving them an advantage? Let them have a go by all means. But there's a big difference between a parent who encourages persistence and effort in a child and one who makes their success in an extra-curricular activity a matter of life and death.

- **Keep it in school:** Steer children towards extra-curricular activities they can do at school, preferably at break or lunchtimes. That way there is no commuting involved, there is more free time and children can get a taste for what they might be good at with less financial pressure.

- **Don't fret over giving up:** Even if children give up instruments or other skills after years of lessons and practice, they have not wasted their time because they will still have learnt a great deal. Remember, too, that children learn from quitting. They learn to admit when they have too much on their plates.

- **Give them a break from competition:** Children need to have friends in a non-competitive atmosphere outside school. They get enough comparison in the classroom without facing more after school hours. Look for courses which teach thinking and life skills, rather than just build CVs, such as yoga or meditation.

- **Hold your nerve:** Leaving our children to their own devices in this day and age has come to be seen as neglectful. But some children are just happier playing at home. Don't assume you are doing nothing by not signing your kids up. See it as making a conscious decision to let them find out more about themselves through play, which is the natural way children learn.

A WORD ON TEENS

THE TEEN YEARS ARE the time when parents really start to panic. Just as our children start to slip out of our control, we become even more impatient for them to measure up and prove their worth with good grades in their GCSEs and A levels.

It is now that we expect a return on our investment and for them to accelerate on a constant onwards and upwards path towards exam glory. As university admissions loom, this means that any little bump on the way feels like a catastrophic car crash.

However, it pays to keep reminding yourself that teens are in a constant state of flux. Their brains are a work in progress, changing at an alarming rate. Scientists have found that the greatest spurts of brain growth after babyhood happen just around adolescence. You can't expect them to have the maturity and drive to behave like a contestant on *The Apprentice* just because you think that's how they need to be to succeed.

At this age, children are less easy to love – and their resistance to our efforts on their behalf and refusal to see the consequences of their actions make it easy to get extremely angry with them. Hold on tight because it will be a bumpy ride. Shaming them and expressing disappointment in their lack of organisation or ambition won't help – and will probably make it worse. Remember that development is not linear. Hormones and immaturity can mean it's a case of two steps forward and one step back. An undesirable trait a teen shows for a month or two might disappear on its own in a matter of weeks. Keep the faith that your child will get there in the end.

In her book *The Blessing of a B Minus*, clinical psychologist Dr Wendy Mogel advises taking the heat out of your relationship with your teen by not discussing university or career choices until they about sixteen or seventeen – even if it means clenching your teeth. By putting that conversation aside until really necessary, it will stop you comparing your child with others and help ease the pressure on them.

Dr Mogel also advises that parents look at their teens with the same unconditional love and understanding they did when their children were toddlers. The stages, after all, are not dissimilar. She says, 'Accepting your teen's individuality and natural evolution is one of the most difficult challenges you'll face as a parent. It means working with, instead of against, your child's unique developmental timetable, endowment, temperament and style.'

FINDING YOUR CHILD'S SPARK

To ENABLE YOUR CHILD to reach their full potential – without needing to be pushed – help them find their 'spark'. This spark is a skill, talent or interest which your child is naturally good at, and which genuinely excites them.

The idea was developed by the late youth-development worker Peter Benson. He explained: 'Every child has a spark – something that is good, beautiful and useful to the world. A spark is something that illuminates a young person's life and gives it energy and purpose.'

It sounds deceptively simple. Yet very few parents sit down and ever ask their children what their passions in life are. Instead we often slip into the habit of pointing children in the direction of skills *we* think will be useful. Often we are so close – and so involved in our own expectations of what they will be good at – that we can't see what really drives a child.

Benson divided sparks into three categories: a skill or talent your child is naturally good at, a commitment such as volunteering or helping the world, or a quality of character, like empathy and listening.

Sparks can be musical, athletic, intellectual, academic or relational; from playing an instrument to helping save animals. They can light the fuse that ignites a career, or balance other activities to make your child feel more whole. They help young people make better use of their time and feel more positive. A spark always draws on an innate talent because kids naturally like to do what they are good at.

To find out what it is, simply ask your child what they love to do. Eight out of ten twelve-year olds already have a good idea straight away. So far children all over the world have identified 220 different sparks.

If your child is still too young to identify it for themselves, watch how they play. Look for the things that absorb and fascinate them or that they naturally gravitate towards when no one else is involved.

Use this knowledge to prune down a child's schedule. Benson said: 'If a teen is involved in a couple of activities that are spark-related, it's much better for them than being involved in a whole bunch of stuff that doesn't really interest them.'

Give your guidance and offer them opportunities to develop it, but resist the temptation to take over. For a child to have real motivation they need to own it for themselves. You can't force inspiration.

Benson believed that when children find their spark, their marks get better, they feel more sense of purpose and they have less conflict with their parents because they feel valued for who they really are – not for who we want them to be.

HOW WE SPEAK TO OUR CHILDREN

W E MAY BELIEVE THAT it's what we do as parents that makes the difference. But just as important is what we say to our children and *how* we say it. We are so powerful in their eyes that every word sends a message, which helps define how they think about themselves.

As kids grow, parents make a huge difference to a child's stress levels – not just by choosing their words carefully but with the tone and body language they use. The words we speak help shape how children relate to themselves, their abilities and the wider world – both positively and negatively. To a sensitive child who is struggling to understand a subject or concept, even remarks like 'Come on, you know the answer' can increase their anxiety about schoolwork – instead of encouraging them.

Furthermore, have you ever caught yourself in full parent mode on video? If so, you may be surprised by the grim expression and the hectoring tones you have slipped into. Even your resting face may convey disappointment to your children – simply because it's blank.

It's easy to assume that if we say the right words, our children will hear the right messages. But around seventy per cent of all meaning is derived from body language. Girls in particular pick up on every single cue we give them. They notice frowns and negative body language more than you think. Instead of barely looking up from your text messages when your child comes home from school, make sure your face really does light up. Use eye contact to show you are listening. Smiling and open body language signal to your child that the world is a safe and calm place. When you are relaxed and happy, they are more likely to feel the same way.

Start noticing how many times a day you smile at your children. Until you start monitoring yourself, you may not realise how much stress and being busy has affected your demeanour. Imagine how your child feels if, most of the time, you appear tense and distracted. But if you break into a grin when you are noticing them doing something right, the positive message will be twice as forceful.

Start seeing yourself from your child's point of view. During homework, it can be intimidating for a small child to have a large grown-up looming over them, while they are desperately trying to think of an answer. If you want to stay in the room, send the message you are helping not judging by pulling up a chair and sitting alongside them. It will send a clear message that you are there to support them, not criticise them.

What to do

- **Use the third person:** To reduce conflict and get a less defensive reaction from your child, use the third person to make it clear it's not about you versus them. Explain, too, why your request is in their interests. Instead of saying 'It's late. Why haven't you started your homework?' try 'It's time to do your homework now. Otherwise you will feel tired tomorrow morning'. Whether we like the consequences or not, most of us have brought our children up to feel they are as much entitled to an opinion as we are. That means that in the same way as adults baulk at being told they 'should', 'must' or that 'they'd better' do something, so do kids. It's not pussyfooting around them – it's simply a way of phrasing a request which is likely to meet less resistance.

- **Don't speak for your children:** One of the classic signs of an over-invested parent is one who often speaks on behalf of their child. Sometimes parents justify it to themselves because they think their child is too modest, is not making their presence felt or needs an advocate. Sometimes children will be shy and ask you to step in. But if you do so without their permission, children can become resentful and angry and feel as if they are being treated like passive projects.

- **Talk about academic subjects at a neutral time:** Schools are now so obsessed with standards that it's unlikely your child will be spared constant assessments of their strengths and weaknesses. Particularly in secondary school, leave it to the teachers as much as possible. If you feel you really must address a child's school performance, choose a quiet, non-confrontational time when your child does not feel

SOME WORDS TO AVOID…

- **Lazy:** This is often shorthand used by parents to describe a child who is not making their best effort. It suggests the child is making a choice and that there is no good reason for a child not to try hard. But often that is very far from the truth, and there will be an underlying reason. These children may have failed so often that they have just given up trying.

- **But:** Even when parents are giving praise, they often can't resist adding a big 'but…' before a suggestion about how their child could do even better next time. The problem is that the word acts like a delete button to cancel out the phrase that came before – so all your child hears is the criticism. If you have something to add, Jenny Foster advises using 'and' to link two thoughts. For example: 'This is a wonderful story *and* it would benefit from proofreading.'

- **If:** Telling your child that *if* they do their homework now, they will get more time to play later makes it sound like it may never happen. Replacing the word 'if' with 'when' shows a clear connection between their own efforts and choices – and the consequences.

- **Try:** The word 'try' implies that the child will fail at whatever is being asked. Instead use a phrase like 'have a go'.

- **Don't:** Begin an instruction with a negative and it gets it off to a bad start. The brain immediately summons up an image of what it can't do rather than what it can. Start a request with a positive suggestion as to how a task can be done so the child immediately sees themselves succeeding at it in their mind's eye.

shamed or defensive. When that moment arises – hopefully when they bring their school work up – ask your child questions rather than tell them how you think they are doing. Don't assume that every child wants to be the top of the class. Some just want to be able

… AND SOME WORDS TO USE

- **Yet:** If a child can't do something, it's usually because they haven't had the chance to learn or practise how to do it. Acknowledge the fact that learning is ongoing and that they will master the task eventually by saying: 'You don't know your six times table *yet*.'

- **Learning:** In classrooms, teachers use the word 'work' ninety-eight per cent of the time and the word 'learning' only two per cent of the time, even though at school they are the same thing. 'Work', however, sounds like a hard slog and not very inviting, while 'learning' sounds like a continual process which is exciting. At home, instead of saying 'Have you done your work?', try saying 'Have you done your learning yet?' Promote the idea that the brain is like a muscle which keeps getting stronger through exercise, the more you use it. Explain how neural pathways are built by practice and repetition and how electrical signals make connections between the nerve cells to form a network. The more the linked cells are used, the stronger the network becomes, forming a memory and eventually a skill.

to cope in a subject that is not their strong point. It's far too much pressure to expect children to be all-rounders – and unless they are perfectionists, many children are happy just to be recognised for their key strengths.

- **Check your tone:** It's not just the words we speak that influence our children. It's also the way in which we express them. One of the most corrosive tones is exasperation, which not only makes a child feel they are a disappointment, but that you have lost faith in their ability. What kind of message is conveyed if it is reinforced with crossed arms, heavy sighing, toe-tapping, and tut-tutting? Even if you are requesting that your child do something they should have already done, or you are repeating yourself, speak in a way in which you'd like to be spoken to. As in all human relationships, the key lies in how you ask.

DROP THE LABELS

LOOK BACK ON YOUR childhood and the labels you were saddled with. It's a good bet that even though they were applied a long time ago, you found it hard to peel them off.

The labels adults apply – both good and bad – can profoundly affect a child's opinion of themselves, especially if they are repeated in their hearing and in public. Common examples include 'clever', 'difficult', 'sporty', 'creative', 'pretty' and 'popular'.

Even if they mostly sound complimentary, they are all damaging in their own way. They can back a child into a corner and restrict your child's freedom to grow and be the person they want to be. In short, they tell a child what to think about themselves. They can also lead them to over-identify with one quality to the detriment of another.

They may also lead children to leave other roles to their siblings. For example, psychologists have found that even among identical twin girls, one sister will identify herself as 'the pretty one' and the other as 'the brainy one'.

One of the key reasons children may underachieve is because another sibling has already cornered the position as the bright one. The other child may assume they are no good at whatever their brother or sister excels at – and then go in search of another domain that they can make their own but which may not do them justice.

SHOW YOUR CHILD THE DIFFERENT WAYS OF BEING INTELLIGENT

For YEARS WE HAVE grown up with the idea that there are only two types of people: academic and non-academic.

The increasing emphasis on tests in today's school system means that even now children are being herded into one of these two camps. IQ-style tests are being used more heavily than ever – often without parents' knowledge. Their use is justified in order to provide baseline levels, below which children are not supposed to fall. But at less enlightened schools, instead of providing a runway for take-off, they are used to justify poor results, and pigeonhole children as high-flyers or low-achievers.

But intelligence quotient is just a small part of what it takes to do well in life. 'A high IQ is like height in a basketball player,' says David Perkins, who studies thinking and reasoning skills at Harvard Graduate School of Education in Cambridge, Massachusetts. 'It is very important, all other things being equal. But all other things aren't equal. There's a lot more to being a good basketball player than being tall, and there's a lot more to being a good thinker than having a high IQ.'

Success in life is based on a large number of different types of intelligence. The work of Robert Sternberg and Howard Gardner has found that traditional methods of measuring intellect are much too narrow and fail to take into account the many different skills that develop and work together in the brain. So tell your child there are of different ways to be clever – and to recognise the unique cocktail of strengths they have – including those that aren't necessarily recognised in classwork or in written exams.

These strengths can include interpersonal intelligence – the ability to read and understand others – and intrapersonal intelligence, or the ability to understand yourself. If your son or daughter is not top of the class in traditional subjects, the fact that future success and happiness is now seen to depend on a unique combination of all these different kinds of intelligence can be hugely encouraging. Show your child you value those qualities just as much. Talk to your kids about people you know with 'street smarts', but not necessarily glowing exam results, who have done well in life – and how the application of perseverance and determination will also take you far.

Help your child to find their learning style, too, so it's easier and more fun – and your child will be working with their brain rather than against it. The three main learning styles are visual – seeing and reading, auditory – hearing and speaking, and kinaesthetic – learning through doing. Ask your child's teacher to find out which style works best for them so that learning is easier.

THE IMPORTANCE OF PLAY

THINK BACK TO YOUR favourite memories of your childhood – and the moments when you felt the most carefree and alive. It could have been when looking down on the world from the branches of a tree, running through the snow or making a den in a hedgerow. It is a good guess that many of your most treasured recollections were when you were outside and playing with no adult supervision.

Children used to have two educations. The one they had at school and the one they had from nature. It was in the moments when we played outdoors, away from adults, that we learnt to think of ourselves as independent beings who could make our own decisions, take our own risks and look after ourselves. We built resilience and self-knowledge through learning what our capabilities were in the wider world.

Yet at the same time as we have heaped the pressures on our own children, we have unwittingly taken away the very tools that enabled us to stand strong and cope with life. Past generations of children have endured worse sources of stress, like war and famine and separation from parents. While the dangers today are not as extreme, they are much more constant.

The irony is that in keeping kids busy with homework, learning apps and extra-curricular activities, we have eroded the downtime they need to deal with and process what they are learning in the classroom. Even if we leave our children alone, they are invariably indoors, distracted by computer games – which increase their adrenalin load even further

– when what they need to be doing is running around and dispersing their stress hormones.

When we were children, being sent to our rooms was the worst punishment we could be given. Now the average child would be delighted by the prospect of uninterrupted time with their phone, laptop or tablet device. In the UK, children are said to be losing contact with nature at a dramatic rate. They are more likely to be able to name a Moshi Monster than a species of bird. The National Trust estimates that in a single generation, since the 1970s, the area around their homes where children are allowed to roam has dropped by ninety per cent.

The phrase 'nature deficit disorders' was coined by author Richard Louv, who argued that the human cost of 'alienation from nature' is the 'diminished use of the senses, attention difficulties and higher rates of physical and emotional illnesses'.

Keeping children indoors like battery hens is interpreted by them to mean they are not to be trusted. If we can't trust them, they feel they cannot trust themselves.

At the same time as children have been spending less time outside, childhood mental disorders have been increasing. It's for this reason that doctors now starting to prescribe exercise instead of drugs. Troubled teenagers are sent to wilderness boot camps to find out who they are because they have never had the chance to find out.

'The chief drawback of children's play,' as Carl Honoré, ambassador for the Slow Movement, points out in his book *Under Pressure*, is that 'to an adult's eye, it looks too much like slacking'. If parents really recognised how much play boosted intellectual development, educators such as Professor David Elkind say they would throw away the Bond papers, sack the tutors and just let their kids get on with it.

Play and learning are not two different things. Studies show that all subjects are best taught through real life and experience rather than textbooks. Children have a much better chance of really understanding science, for example, if they spend time in nature, so they can see how key concepts like the changing state of matter, forces and photosynthesis work in the real world.

When in 2011 Unicef asked children their requirements for

happiness they named time with families, friends and the outdoors.

Author Jay Griffiths looked at how contemporary society is denying children the time, space and place to be children, with serious consequences, in her book *Kith*. Griffiths says: 'Studies show that when children are allowed unstructured play in nature, their sense of freedom, independence and inner strength all thrive, and children who are surrounded by nature are not only less stressed but also bounce back from the stressful events more readily.'

Play was mankind's first form of education. It was the philosopher and psychologist Karl Groos who was among the first modern thinkers to suggest that play is a preparation for later life. In his 1898 book he pointed out that when animals play, they are practising survival skills. All the young of mammals play. The differences between the games of puppies and kittens and baby apes show that they practise the skills they need the most. Antelope play at running and dodging, while young tigers practise pouncing and stalking. By taking away play, we take away our children's very survival skills.

One generation of high-stakes testing cannot socialise human children – who were reared for millennia to be hunter-gatherers – out of the basic need to go foraging, climb trees and build dens. But then in the middle of the twentieth century, adults started to get involved by turning play into sport and extra-curricular activities, based on the fear that children could not be trusted to play on their own.

Teachers increasingly believe that the reason they are seeing more behaviour issues in the classroom, as well as bullying, is that children have less opportunity to work out their issues – and learn how to behave. When children play games, they learn how to compromise, make up rules, think creatively and learn which behaviour is acceptable to others and which is not. There are no right answers.

So try backing off. Allow them to get bored and go outside. Instead of drawing up a schedule, just be 'quietly available'. Child psychologist Dr Pat Spungin calls such under-parenting 'benign neglect', which is just another way of saying 'don't interfere until they start putting the dog in fancy dress'.

WHAT TO LOOK FOR IN A SCHOOL

FIRST, LEAVE YOUR EGO at the school gate. Your child's school is not a status symbol. It's supposed to be the right fit for your child.

I have seen parents beat down the doors of schools they were determined their children would go to, because if they were honest with themselves, it would give them bragging rights. But if you are having to tutor your child, or squeeze them in, it's probably not the right place – or your child is not what they are looking for. It doesn't mean your child is failing – simply that it's not the right match.

If you go ahead and force your child in anyway, be aware that they may not thrive – and unless there is some truly thoughtful, progressive teaching in place, that failure can quickly become self-reinforcing. Confidence shattered in primary school can take a long time to rebuild. One recent London School of Economics study found that boys in particular can be held back for years if they have been ranked poorly.

If you are applying for private school, seeing which school comes highest in the league table should not be your main criterion. Researchers say that some children are better off going to a less academically high-flying school where they will perform relatively better.

There are no GCSEs in character. But look for schools that teach it anyway. Over the last five years, for example, Wellington College pupils have been asked to learn five values; courage, integrity, kindness, responsibility and respect and it's probably more than a happy coincidence that exam performance there has also rocketed from sixty-five per cent A and B grade at A level to ninety-three per cent. While few of us have the money for a school like this, there really are other places starting to follow these principles too. Of course, in attempting to attract new customers, all private schools will claim to produce a well-rounded child – often sticking a picture of a pupil playing a violin on the front of the prospectus as if that proves their commitment. But by 'well-rounded', many schools actually mean *all-rounders*. For any school to produce a truly well-rounded child, they need to cultivate values, qualities and skills that are not recognised by exam results, rather than just pay lip service to them.

By all means look for schools with strong pastoral care. But is it proactive, helping children to learn the emotional tools they need to cope in life? Or is it reactive, where they have to provide counselling and care for swathes of pupils already falling by the wayside because of the competitive, exam-obsessed atmosphere?

Find out, too, how a school responds if a child is struggling. Do teachers try to help pupils who need help with extra sessions at lunchtime or after school? Or do they bat the problem back into the parents' court, putting children on 'red lists', telling parents to pay for tutoring – and then, if that does not work, informing them that the school was not right for their child after all.

A sure sign of whether a school is truly interested in the welfare of its pupils is how many children it eases out at key stages and particularly in the run-up to public exams, a process that has come to be known as 'academic cleansing'. Schools will always trot out the mantra: 'We are only doing what is right for the child.' The truth is that these schools are usually doing what is right for their league table results. As David Levin, previously headmaster of City of London School, points out: 'It is basically treating children as expendable in order to boost your position on the league tables… It is immoral.'

Look for a school for your child that, as much as possible, reminds you of the principles that work in Finland: excellent, highly trained, energetic teachers; lots of autonomy for staff in the classroom; a focus on cooperation, not competition; facilities that show non-academic subjects are valued; and a commitment to teaching pupils how to think, not just what to learn.

Most of all, look to the head. Ultimately it starts – and ends – with them. What is their philosophy of education? Are they running a school like a business based around results? Do they tend to have a fixed view of children's abilities and want pupils who give them as little extra work as possible – or do they moan that they can only work with what they get? Do they have a track record of moving children out of the school rather than helping to address the core difficulties a child is having? Do they really value good teaching and ease out those who are not stimulating children or helping them reach their potential? Are you allowed to contact your child's teachers directly if you are worried about anything – or are you kept at arm's length? Really understanding the ethos of the schools you apply for could make a huge difference to your child's experience of education.

When talking to your child, value every type of school, not just the ones with the high-flying results, so they don't feel that going anywhere else is 'second best'. There are probably a few schools that would be a good fit for your child. Don't just make one the be-all-and-end-all – or the pressure on your child will become intolerable.

The same goes when your teenager is applying for university. Look at what the courses will offer your child, not just how much kudos they will bring. In the UK, there are plenty of other universities that offer the same top-flight education as Oxbridge, yet even graduates of establishments like Durham, Bristol and London feel they live with the life-long stigma of being Oxbridge 'rejects'.

CONCLUSION

'Education is not the learning of facts, but
the training of the mind.'

Albert Einstein

'The principle goal of education in the schools should be
creating men and women who are capable of doing new
things, not simply repeating what other generations have
done; men and women who are creative, inventive and
discoverers, who can be critical and verify, and not accept
everything they are offered.'

Jean Piaget

'If your child has a talent to be a baker,
do not ask him to be a doctor.'

Hasidic proverb

THE HOLY GRAIL AT the end of this long journey is of course a place at a top university. To get there, most young people will have had to have also turned themselves into walking résumés, at the expense of their childhoods.

So why, after trying so hard to get to this point, do so many find it hard to adjust? Is it just a coincidence that the more elite the institution, the harder students find it to cope?

Positive psychologist Shawn Achor, a former counsellor at Harvard, observed that after the initial euphoria of arriving at the world-famous institution wore off, students quickly came down to earth with a bump. Even though they had made it to the very top of the competitive tree, having beaten tens of thousands of young people around the world, there was still no satisfaction. Instead they now realised they had to focus on the next contest: how to keep up with a new set of peers who were just as clever. Achor says an astonishing eighty per cent became depressed as a result.

We know that these are not the children of absent, neglectful parents and have perhaps never wanted for anything. On the contrary, their parents would have been there to love and support them every step of the way. Yet officials at US universities have nicknames for their undergraduates. They call them 'teacups' – students who have been so overprotected they are breakable – or 'crispies' – pressured so much they have burnt out. In other words, the product of all this parental investment may, if you are lucky, be academic accolades galore. But these young people appear to be a long way from being the strong, resilient leaders of the future.

In the UK, too, the outcomes are similar. Even though they have also reached our idea of the educational pinnacle, fifteen to twenty per cent of Cambridge students seek counselling. The number at Oxford who need support is also climbing. In universities across the country, one in ten students surveyed by the National Union of Students had suicidal thoughts while at their current college. Figures from the Office of National Statistics found a fifty per cent increase in the number of students who had gone on to kill themselves between 2007 and 2011.

A generation ago, students still believed that the world was their oyster. Now armies of young people are graduating from courses with qualifications for jobs which are not there. Until now, the idea of graduates working for nothing would have seemed laughable. Now they do so – despite having student debts hanging over their heads.

Yet material and academic success is really the only thing we tell our children to aim for. No wonder they are despondent and exhausted. Over the next ten years, the number of children with symptoms of a mental disorder is expected to double. As psychologist Madeline Levine, who treats young people who are casualties of the system, points out, the result is 'a generation of kids who resemble nothing so much as trauma victims…They are anxious and depressed and often self-medicate with drugs and alcohol. Sleep is difficult and they walk around in a fog of exhaustion. Other kids simply fold their cards and refuse to play.'

Even if it only survived for a short-lived period, the benign but adventurous 'Blue Peter' ideal of childhood in which children are allowed to find the time to develop at their own pace through play and self-discovery has gradually been lost. Instead we have introduced constant comparison to make children work harder and 'do better', creating a socially toxic environment.

Children who are in a never-ending race to compare themselves in all areas have brittle confidence, because this is not a warm and welcoming world in which to grow and find out who they are. Instead it turns childhood into a battle on all fronts.

Despite all their privileges, middle-class children suffer in their own way because they are expected to do well. They have no excuse not to. On paper they get better opportunities so when it does not work out, they feel they have no one to blame but themselves, turning their feelings inwards. Those who never had the chances or parental backing fare little better, feeling they are losers before the race even begins. Tragically, as many as three-quarters of a million of these young people who are not in work or training after leaving school in the UK feel they 'have nothing to live for' according to a study for the Prince's Trust charity.

Studies show that adults tend to feel good about their achievements

– until they are shown the examples of others who have achieved more. Then they become depressed. If grown-ups cannot rationalise or see their attainments in context, how much harder must it be for children? Even if they do succeed, they don't have to look far in this world of social comparison to be shown examples of someone else doing better.

Of course, it is not parents' fault that society is now organised along these lines. Nor is it the teachers' fault that they have to feed a monster of an education system with high-flying exam results – or be considered 'failing' themselves. Everything in our world – from the richest and most beautiful people to the schools and universities – is now organised by lists, leagues and tables or 'best' or 'worst', even if the methods of that judgement are completely arbitrary or superficial. We once lived in smaller communities where it was possible to be a big fish in a small pond – and the number of people to compete with was limited. Now most of us feel like we are drowning in an ocean.

But even though we parents are also victims of this culture of comparison – and suffer from it every day ourselves in different contexts – we have allowed ourselves also to get swept up in it, and have passed those pressures down to our children. Instead of being a buffer against it, we have permitted ourselves to be ranked by the successes of our sons and daughters. Yes, we must set standards for our children. But they should be for effort and originality, not just attainment. Yes, we must help them reach their potential, but one that is consistent with their innate skills and personality. Children naturally arrive on the planet with different aptitudes and – while these can be developed – there is no point in seeking the same one-size-fits-all goal of a professional, graduate career for all of them. Whether your child has a place at Oxford or a place on a manual apprenticeship course, we must treat both with equal respect because, as Levine says, 'both of these options carry the possibility of success and neither guarantees it'.

It's already tough enough out there for kids, without us parents making it tougher. It is so obvious that nothing is more important for children than mental well-being that it hardly bears saying – except that it seems to have been forgotten. Over the last few decades, we have made huge strides forward in animal rights and sexual and racial equality. But although our children are more legally protected than ever and safer from physical harm, they are also more vulnerable. The threat has moved indoors – into homes and classrooms – and parents, teachers and politicians have unwittingly become their gaolers.

Those with the best exam results are deemed the winners, even though the real question, as educationalist Ken Robinson puts it, is not 'how intelligent are you, but how are you intelligent?' Although we continually strive to make our children cleverer, we have yet to teach our children the lesson that 'none of us is as smart as all of us'. Child labour was once considered instrumental to the success of the Industrial Revolution. Now, after a brief reprieve, children are being roped in as infantry in another global economic war – with little consideration of the personal price they will pay.

How confusing it must be for a child today. On the one hand we parents endlessly tell them they are special. We reinforce the message that they must be unique to get ahead. On the other, we allow them to be dehumanised by marching them through a shape-sorter exam system which is devised primarily to arm them for the battle ahead.

There is of course a huge imbalance of power here. Children are in our hands. They have little say. Their only outlet is to express their unhappiness through misery or rebellion. However, our future lies with the next generation. Their well-being is more essential now then ever as the human race faces challenges, like climate change and overpopulation, which will require cooperation, not competition. More than ever, we need to raise our sons and daughters on better principles than the need to beat everyone in their class, or for their school to beat every other in the borough, or their nation to defeat every other country on Earth.

In short, we have to be careful what we wish for. Mental equilibrium, not exam certificates, should be the real measure of our success as parents.

Already there are changes afoot. Around the world, parents and educators are drawing up a blueprint for an alternative. Whether it's slow parenting, minimalist parenting, free-range parenting – or the more bluntly named calm the f*** down parenting – there is recognition that we need to resist the impulse to micromanage.

The change starts with you, letting go bit by bit. We need to set aside our ideas of what our children are 'supposed to be' – and let them be what they are. Most of all, we need to appreciate how wonderful our children are in their own way – even if it's not in the way we once wanted them to be.

It can only happen one child at a time. But starting with your own family, by seeking out different schools, and demonstrating different priorities, you will be one step closer to restoring the equilibrium. Furthermore you will not only be taming your inner tiger, you will also be freeing your child.

As for my own children, Lily and Clio, I love the fact that when they come home from school now and I ask them 'How are you?' I really mean it. It's no longer code for: 'What marks did you get today?' Most of all, I love the fact that I can finally appreciate my daughters for who they are – funny, quirky girls who love their pets, hot chocolate, Converse trainers and walks in the park. It's up to them what they want to do with their future. I can only step aside and hope they will live up to their personal bests. Not mine.

NOTES

INTRODUCTION

Interviews with Dana Wilkey from author's own interview from 'Can you teach your baby to read?', *Daily Mail*, 12 December 2012.

Criticism of 'Your Baby Can Read': See Federal Trade Commission rules 'Baby Can Read Ads Deceptive', Judith Keer, Associated Press, 28 August 2012.

'Autumn babies more likely to get into Oxbridge: Are school odds stacked against summer babies?', Sean Coughlan, BBC News, based on Freedom of Information request which showed the chances of going to Oxford or Cambridge are thirty per cent higher for babies born in autumn rather than summer, 24 July 2013.

See also: 'Don't come out yet, baby – I want you to be top of the class: The mothers who'll do ANYTHING to have September birth,' Clare Goldwin, *Daily Mail*, 28 August 2013.

Young children increasingly suffering anxiety from academic pressure: From author's interview with Jenny Foster.

British children in sixteenth place out of twenty-one countries for well-being: UNICEF Report Card 11 – Child well-being in rich countries, April 2013. (The previous report card put them last.)

Statistics on children's unhappiness: A study of 30,000 young people aged eight to sixteen suggested that half a million people in that age group are actively unhappy. Good Childhood Report, published by The Children's Society, 2012.

More than 80,000 children estimated to suffer from a severe form of depression: National Institute of Clinical Excellence report, 'Care and support for children and young people with depression needs to be improved', 17 September 2013.

Suicide is the second most common cause of death among fifteen- to nineteen-year-olds after road traffic accidents: 'Pushing Children to Breaking Point', Adi Bloom, *The Times Educational Supplement*, 19 April 2013.
    Self-harm calls to ChildLine show biggest increase: Sean Coughlan, BBC News website, 5 December 2012, based on ChidLine figures.

Growth in depression among teenagers: World Health Organisation says adolescents in the developed world have the fastest-growing incidence of mental health problems on the planet. See WHO website.

Seven out of ten people now view themselves as belonging to Middle Britain compared with a quarter a generation ago: *Daily Telegraph*, based on research by Britain Thinks, 20 March 2011.

PART ONE: How tiger parenting became a global force

Babies under six months should never be played with: Extracts of agony aunt letters taken from *Never Kiss a Man in a Canoe*, Tanith Carey, Boxtree Macmillan, 2009.

You have to start them young and push them on toward their goal: Interviews with Linda Hale and paediatricians from 'Parents are pushing their kids to learn earlier than ever. How smart is it?', *Newsweek*, Langway, Jackson, Shirley and Whitmore, 28 March 1983.

Coining of the term 'baby burn-out': 'Too much stimulation can lead to baby burn-out', Agence France Presse, 13 April 2000.

One-half of all literacy problems came from children being pushed to read before they were ready: For more from Professor Elkind, see his book *The Hurried Child* (25th anniversary edition), Da Capo Press, 1 February 2007.

Baby Einstein DVD fails to boost language: *Reuters Health*, March 2010, based on study published in *Archives of Pediatrics & Adolescent Medicine*. Also 'Baby Einsteins: Not So Smart After All', Alice Park, *Time Magazine*, August 2007.

Disney refunds parents for Baby Einstein DVDs following legal threats: *Brand Republic*, 28 October 2009.

Children under two should not watch TV: Recommendations on TV viewing for young children from the American Academy of Pediatrics http://www.aap.org/en-us/advocacy-and-policy/aap-health-initiatives/pages/media-and-children.aspx.

Baby videos don't make your baby cleverer: 'Want a Brainier Baby? Loading up on tapes, games and videos may not be a smart move', Pamela Paul, *Time Magazine*, January 2006. See also 'Wishful Thinking: Many Parents Believe That Watching Videos and DVDs May Help Bring Out the Budding Genius in Their Babies', Sandra G. Boodman, *Washington Post*, 9 October 2007.

Baby videos decrease vocabulary: 'Associations Between Media Viewing and Language Development in Children Under Age Two Years', F Zimmerman,

Dimitri Chistakis, Andrew Melzoff, University of Washington, published in the *Journal of Pediatrics*, 2007. It must be noted that Julie Aigner-Clark and her husband continue to dispute this study, saying they found correspondence in the research which raised concerns over the way the findings were analysed. After requesting the records, the University of Washington settled with the Clarks, paying out nearly $200,000 in back legal fees. In 2013, the data was checked again by independent scholars who concluded it was safest to suggest that baby videos had minimal impact on language development, but it was not proven that they decreased it.

Early learning could slow down development through neurological 'crowding': Peter Huttenlocher in *Nurturing a Healthy Mind: Doing What Matters Most for Your Child's Developing Brain*, Michael C. Nagel, Exisle Publishing, 2012. See also Kathy Hirsh-Pasek in her book *Einstein Never Used Flashcards: How Our Children Really Learn—And Why They Need to Play More and Memorize Less*, Rodale Press, 31 August 2004.

Being a pushy parent has little effect on your child – babies filter out information they see as too complicated: Richard Aslin of the Rochester Baby Lab, University of Rochester, quoted in the *Daily Mail*, 23 May 2012.

Children learn best from human interaction: Celeste Kidd quoted from 'Babies' Hunger to Learn has a "Goldilocks Effect"', Sindya Bhanoo, *New York Times*, 29 May 2012.

Too many toys, activities and outings hampering a baby's ability to focus: *Early Intelligence*, Lise Eliot, Penguin Press Science, 2001.

The more stress hormones swarm babies' brains, the less likely they are to succeed intellectually: *Brain Rules for Babies: How to Raise a Smart and Happy Child from Zero to Five*, John Medina, Pear Press, 2011. See also www.brainrules.net.

Toy industry has not proved that apps make babies cleverer: 'Toy industry eager to defend baby apps, but science is scant', Cecilia Kang, *Washington Post*, 15 August 2013.

48,000 developers developing apps for children: The Association for Competitive Technology, which represents developers. See actonline.org.

NATURE VERSUS NATURE: CAN WE 'CREATE' OUR CHILDREN?

Genes contribute about fifty per cent to a child's intelligence; GCSE results 'influenced by children's genes, not teaching': Children's exam results are largely a product of their genes and not standards of teaching in schools, according to a new study that could have a major bearing on future education policy, *Daily Telegraph*, Graeme Paton, 25 July 2013.

Hundreds of genes contribute to intelligence: 'Huge scan of the human genome finds no single gene that has an appreciable effect on intelligence', *New Scientist*, Andy Coghlan, December 1, 2007.

Why genes could explain why some children never perform well in exams while others sail through: A study by Dr Chang Chun-yen, Director of the Science Education Centre at National Taiwan Normal University in Taipei, compared scores on the National Basic Competency Test of 779 young teenagers from four schools with each student's COMT genetic make-up. Students with two copies of a mutation called Met-158, which clears dopamine more slowly, tend to have a better working memory and higher verbal IQs than students with one or two copies of a mutation called Val-158, which clears dopamine from the synapses faster. *South China Morning Post*, Anjali Hazari, 19 August 2013.

How genes influence a child's temperament and their response to parenting: 'A sensitive child? It's all in the genes', *The Times*, based on study by Ben Hankin of the University of Denver, published in the journal *Translational Psychiatry*, October 2011.

Do children inherit their parents' IQ? Estimations of heritability of intelligence based on a lecture given by Steve Hsu, University of Oregon, 18 August 2011: http://www.youtube.com/watch?v=62jZENi1ed8

IQ rising by three points a decade: *Are We Getting Smarter? Rising IQ in the Twenty-First Century*, James R. Flynn, Cambridge University Press, 2012.

THE RISE OF THE TUTOR

A quarter of school children now get tutoring: A poll by Ipsos MORI for the Sutton Trust shows that twenty-four per cent of all young people in 2013 said they had received private or home tuition at some stage in their school career, compared with eighteen per cent in 2005 and twenty-three per cent in 2012, www.suttontrust.com.

Parents spend £6bn a year on private tuition: 'A quarter of parents use private tutors, labelling school support as "inadequate"', Emma Wall, *Daily Telegraph*, 2 November 2012.

Tutoring is all about parental anxiety: Barry Sindall quotes from 'Time for the Private Tutor', *Management Today*, 8 July 2013.

Tutoring trades on insecurity about exams: Clarissa Farr quotes from 'Poorer parents digging deep to fund boom in private tutoring'; 'Minority ethnic families also behind huge rise'; 'Heads say agencies are trading on insecurity', Jessica Shepherd, *Guardian*, 27 April 2013.

Tutoring is the 'Wild West' of education: Sion Humphreys quoted from Radio 4 documentary, Teacher Versus Tutor, 2 August 2013.

Tutors discount pupils' needs: Author's interview with Carolyn Kerr.

Tutors may not understand pupils' difficulties: Author's interview with Noël Janis-Norton.

BE CAREFUL WHAT YOU WISH FOR PART ONE:

THE JAPANESE EXPERIENCE

Murder of Haruna Wakayama: 'A Child's Killing Startles Japanese; Case Reflects Pressure To Succeed in Schools', Kathryn Tolbert, *Washington Post*, 27 November 1999.

The culture of 'school envy': 'Japan's government urges ceasefire in kindergarten exam wars', Makiko Tazaki, Agence France Presse, 30 November 1999.

'Murder trial has Japan worried about mothers' troubled lives', Scott Stoddard, Associated Press, 6 March 2000.

'Kanagawa woman gets 4 years in prison for killing son', *Japan Weekly Monitor*, 27 February 2006.

Western views of Japanese education: *Education in Japan: Competing Visions for the Future*, Christopher Bjork and Ryoko Tsuneyoshi, Phi Delta Kappan, 1 April 2005.

Envy of Japanese education in the West: 'Asian Students Excelling in Area, US Schools', Lawrence Feinberg, *Washington Post*, 21 July 1981.

Soul-searching among Japanese on the causes of the problems with their young people: 'Are they the problem or are we?', Masami Ito, *Japan Times*, 5 May 2002.

Rising violence in Japanese schools: 'Youth Violence Has Japan Struggling for Answers'; '11-Year-Old's Killing of Classmate Puts Spotlight on Sudden Acts of Rage', Anthony Faiola, *Washington Post*, 9 August 2004.

Japan's suicide rate: 'World's suicide capital – tough image to shake', Eric Prideaux, *Japan Times*, 20 November 2007. See also '90 suicides a day spur Japan into action', *Leo Lewis, The Times*, 12 November 2007.

Japanese husbands avoid going home: 'Home Avoidance Syndrome', discussed by Michael Hirsh, Associated Press, 27 January 1991.

Scaling back testing like 'going to war without weapons': *Education in Japan: Competing Visions for the Future*, *ibid*.

Hikikomori discussed in 'Japan's Crisis of the Mind', Masaru Tamamato, *International Herald Tribune*, 2 March 2009.

BE CAREFUL WHAT YOU WISH FOR PART TWO: CHINA

Before *Battle Hymn of the Tiger Mother*, there was *Harvard Girl*: 'Best Sellers Reflecting Chinese's Life Interests', Xinhua general news service, 21 November 2001.

Shanghai shoots to number one on world education league tables: PISA rankings can be found at www.oecd.org/pisa/46643496.pdf.

Response to league tables: As President Barack Obama said in his 2011 State of the Union address: 'We know what it takes to compete for the jobs and industries of our time. We need to out-innovate, out-educate, and out-build the rest of the world.'

'PISA slip should put a rocket under our world-class ambitions and drive us to win the education space race', Michael Gove, *The Times Educational Supplement*, 17 December 2010.

'Stagnant' UK on the slide in world education rankings: Gove admits he is 'daunted by scale of challenge', Jessica Shepherd, *Guardian*, 8 December 2010.

'Britain has turned into the thick man of Europe', Tariq Tahir, *Metro*, 8 December 2010.

'Bottom of the class': 'UK literacy and numeracy standards slip down international rankings', Richard Garner, *Independent*, 4 December 2013.

'Crackdown on South Korean Cram Schools', Michael Alison Chandler, *Washington Post*, 4 April 4 2011.

'Shining natural light on myopia in China', David Pierson, *Los Angeles Times*, 5 July 2012, based on three-year trial in Guangzhou, China by Ian Morgan, visiting professor at the Zhongshan Ophthalmic Center.

'Chinese children sickened by school pressure', Agence France Presse, based on a study of 2,191 pupils aged nine to twelve by Therese Hesketh, a professor at University College London. According to the study, seventy-three percent had been physically punished by their parents, 18 January 2010.

China's strength in PISA study highlights schools' weakness: Andreas Landwehr, Deutsche Presse-Agentur, 16 December 2010.

How Chinese schools are not producing creative students: 'Flunking innovation and creativity: East Asia's highly touted test scores in math, science, and reading are masking important failures in developing innovators and entrepreneurs', Yong Zhao, Phi Delta Kappan, 1 September 2012.

The growing Waldorf education movement in China: 'A return to the spirit and soul', Rose Garrett, *Lilipoh* magazine, 22 March 2012. Ze Wu, who taught in public schools for twelve years before discovering Waldorf education, says that Chinese children as young as nine years old have committed suicide from the academic pressure. He says many people know the education system in China is broken but no one knows how to fix it.

Rise in home schooling in China: 'Experts discuss the benefits of home schooling', Jin Zhu, *China Daily* (European Edition), 25 August 2013.

'Academic Pressure Too Much For Some Kids', Feng Yu, *Global Times*, 13 December 2013.

How Chinese students view their education: 'Conflict in Chinese Education: Students' ambivalence toward their experiences in secondary education: Views from a group of young Chinese studying on an international foundation program in Beijing', Alex Cockain, *China Journal*, January 2011.

China's concerns about shortcomings of education system: Via psychologist Professor Peter Gray, 2013, of Boston Collage in *Aeon* magazine: 'In an article entitled "The Test Chinese Schools Still Fail" in the *Wall Street Journal* in December 2010, Jiang Xueqin, a prominent Chinese educator, wrote: "The failings of a rote-memorisation system are well known: lack of social and practical skills, absence of self-discipline and imagination, loss of curiosity and passion for learning…One way we'll know we're succeeding in changing China's schools is when those scores [on standardised tests] come down." Meanwhile, Yong Zhao, an American education professor who grew up in China and specialises in comparing the Chinese educational system with the system in the US, notes that a common term used in China to refer to graduates is *gaofen dineng*, meaning "high scores but low ability".' See also Gray's book *Free To Learn*, Basic Books, 2013.

ANOTHER WAY?

How Finland's education system fares so well: *The Finland Phenomenon: Inside the World's Most Surprising School System, a film by Bob Compton*, New School Films, http://www.youtube.com/watch?v=bcC2l8zioIw.

The well-being of Finland's children: UNICEF's child well-being tables, http://www.unicef.org.uk/Images/Campaigns/FINAL_RC11-ENG-LORES-fnl2.pdf.

DOES COMPETITION MAKE CHILDREN DO BETTER?

For a complete exploration of this topic, see *No Contest: the Case Against Competition*, Alfie Kohn, Houghton Mifflin, 1993.

Competition can interfere with thinking: Scans of people trying to solve puzzles have found that the fear centres in their brains are more likely to be activated when players are told they are competing. From 'The neural bases of cooperation and competition: an MRI investigation', Jean Decety, Philip L. Jackson, Jessica A. Sommerville, Thierry Chaminade, Andrew N. Meltzoff, *NeuroImage* 23, 2004.

Children are taught to be competitive by the societies they live in: In the March 1998 issue of *Share International* magazine, Kohn describes how children are socialised by their societies to be competitive. He cites a study comparing Anglo-American children raised in the US, Mexican children raised in the US and children raised in Mexico who have had no contact with US culture. It was found that all four- and five-year-olds will help one another take turns in winning. But among seven- to ten-year-olds, both Anglo-American and Mexican-American children prevent anyone from winning fifty to eighty per cent of the time. Only Mexican seven- to nine-year-olds with little or no contact with American culture managed to cooperate and earn prizes in a majority of the games.

Children are more creative when they are told it's not a competition: 'A growing body of research suggests that the old carrot-on-a-stick approach may actually stifle performance', Alfie Kohn, *Los Angeles Times*, 4 December 1989. In this article Kohn describes how Harvard Business School psychologist Teresa Amabile carried out numerous experiments to find the conditions which helped creativity flourish – and those which harmed it. During her work she has asked people across a wide range of ages to do something imaginative, like make collage or write poems and short stories. She found that those who were told their efforts were *not* going to be judged or entered into competitions were found by a panel of experts to produce the most daring and imaginative work.

BENDING THE RULES: WHY CHEATING IS ON THE RISE

Rise in number of cheating students: Nearly 1,700 students at 20 leading UK institutions were disciplined for academic misconduct in the year 2010/2011 alone, according to figures released under the Freedom of Information Act. Around 100 were expelled.

'First-class essay? Yours for just £660; Business is booming for "private tutors" who write students' essays for them', Christopher Middleton, *Daily Telegraph*, 7 December 2011.

'Win at all costs: most children admit to cheating at sport', Richard Garner, *Independent*, 15 April 2013, based on survey of over 1,000 children by the Marylebone Cricket Club.

'Drug tests on way for students as one in 10 use exam boosters'; 'Senior academics also admit using "cognitive enhancers" such as Ritalin to improve memory', Steve Connor, *Independent*, 7 November 2012.

Chinese universities ban bras: 'Bid to crack down on cheating in "world's toughest exam"', 7 July 2013, based on a report in *China Daily Online*.

Why testing creates a culture of cheating: Professor Eric Anderman on how testing culture creates more cheating in 'Cheating Upwards; Stuyvesant kids do it. Harvard kids do it. Smart kids may especially do it. But why?', Robert Kolker, *New York Magazine*, 24 September 2012.

Parents taking part in cheating: 'Got a headache? It'll boost your GCSE grade: Record number of schoolchildren see scores increased by claiming illness during exams', Wills Robinson, *Mail Online*, 31 October 2013, based on figures released by exam watchdog Ofqual.

'Massive rise in parents caught lying to win a top school place', Sarah Harris, *Daily Mail*, 26 February 2013. Based on Freedom of Information requests to all 152 local education authorities in England on fraudulent applications for primary and secondary schools between 2007/8 and 2013/14.

'How testing culture makes cheating more likely', from *Mindset: How You Can Fulfil Your Potential*, Carol Dweck, Robinson, 2012.

The rise in homeschooling in the UK: 'The Review of Elective Home Education', Children, Schools and Families Committee, 2009. For the rise in the US, see the US Institute of Education Sciences.

PART TWO – How competitive parenting and schooling affect our children

One in ten children between the ages of one and fifteen has a mental health disorder. Source: The Office for National Statistics, 'Mental health in children and young people in Great Britain, 2005'. Also see 'One in 10 children suffers mental illness', Rebecca Smith, *Evening Standard*, 20 June 2006. The British Medical Association also estimates that one in ten children under the age of fifteen is suffering from mental illness ranging from depression to obsessive disorders.

Reports by NCH, the children's charity, also say that one in ten children has a mental health disorder to a 'clinically significant' level.

First signs of mental illness show by fourteen: Half of those with lifetime mental health problems first experience symptoms by the age of fourteen, and three-quarters before their mid-twenties. Source: Mental Health Outcomes Strategy, NHS Choices.

'Teens own £5k of stuff', *Mirror*, 14 January 2010, from a survey by home insurers esure.

Exam stress among children: 'Helping youngsters cope with the pressure of exam season'; 'It's exam season – as ChildLine launches a campaign to help children suffering from exam stress', Hannah Stephenson, *Western Morning News*, 7 May 2013.

'Testing times – following the suicide of a 15-year-old student last week, what can parents do to ease the pressure of exams?', Diane Taylor, *Guardian*, 2 June 2004.

Affluent children suffering more anxiety: Children from homes with an annual income of more than £100,000 a year were found to be suffering anxiety and depression at twice the normal rate of their less well-off peers, based on a study by American psychologist Suniya Luthar of Arizona State University published in the *Journal of Development and Psychopathology* and *Psychology Today*, November 2013.

'"Toxic childhoods" blamed for 22,000 self-harm cases'; 'Children self-harming as a way of coping with stress', Laura Donnelly, *Daily Telegraph*, 2 October 2013, based on NHS figures.

Primary schools turning to relaxation techniques: 'Just Chilled to Perfection: A New Brighton primary school has cracked the art of relaxation', Ben Turner, *Liverpool Daily Echo*, 19 January 2010.

How stress leads to workplace absence: Figures from 'Work-Related Stress: a guide', Health and Safety Executive, http://www.hse.gov.uk/stress/pdfs/eurostress.pdf.

Children suffering stress due to SATs: 'Primary pupils missing meals over SATs stress'; 'Children can't concentrate because they're worried', Katy Hallam, *Birmingham Mail*, 15 May 2013.

Extent of school phobia: 'One fifth of British children suffer from "school phobia" but half of parents are unaware of the problem', Mario Ledwith, *Daily Mail*, 19 February 2013, based on 1,054 parents polled by 'This Morning' and the parenting website Netmums.

Girls being asked to do too much: Professor Carrie Paechter of Goldsmiths, University of London, speaking at the Girls' Schools Association Annual Conference, November 2012.

'Why do children self-harm? Teenagers who cut themselves are too often dismissed as looking for attention. But their distress is real, and their numbers are growing', Kate Hilpern, *Independent*, 13 October 2013.

Interview with Rachel Welch of selfharm.co.uk, by the author.

Why middle-class children are particularly at risk: *The Price of Privilege: How Parental Pressure and Material Advantage Are Creating a Generation of Disconnected and Unhappy Kids*, Madeline Levine, Harper Perennial, 2008. Soniya Luthar study. *Ibid*.

Starting children young: Quotes from Cathy Brown from 'Crème de la Crème: They've only just begun'; 'Preschool proms take aim at dropout rates. Youngsters get a taste of what to expect as high school seniors', D. Aileen Dodd, *Atlanta Journal-Constitution*, May 1, 2010.

Social media increasing pressure: Author's interview with Deanne Jade of the National Centre for Eating Disorders, www.eating-disorders.org.uk.

Suicides among young people: Figures from the Samaritans, http://www.samaritans.org/website. See also interview with Alastair Sharp, from 'Pushing children to breaking point', Adi Bloom, *The Times Educational Supplement*, 19 April 2013.

Does early academic focus pay off? Comparison of children in academically focused nurseries and non-academic nurseries: *Einstein Never Used Flashcards: How Our Children Really Learn—And Why They Need to Play More and Memorize Less*, Kathy Hirsh-Pasek and Roberta Golinkoff, Rodale, 2004.

Why early reading does not give a head start: 'Rush, Little Baby—How the push for infant academics may actually be a waste of time—or worse', Neil Swidey, *Boston Globe*, 28 October 2007. A study in the 1930s by noted researcher and Illinois educator Carleton Washburne compared the trajectories of children who had begun reading at several ages, up to seven. Washburne concluded that, in general, a child could best learn to read beginning around the age of six. By middle school, he found no appreciable difference in reading levels between the kids who had started young versus the kids who had started later, except the earlier readers appeared to be less motivated and less excited about reading. More recent research also raises doubt about the push for early readers. See also the *Elementary School Journal*, vol. 31, no. 7, March 1931. A cross-cultural study of European children published in 2003 in the *British Journal of Psychology* found that those taught to read at age five had more reading problems than those who were taught at age seven. The findings supported a 1997 report critical of Britain's early-reading model.

One in ten children of primary-school age are estimated to be affected by poor comprehension: See 'Supporting Children with Reading and Comprehension Impairments', Economic and Social Research Council, Dr Paula Clarke, York University.

HOW LEAGUE TABLES HAVE CHANGED OUR SCHOOLS

The birth of league tables: 'Who are headmasters helping by withholding exam results? John Clare, who invented school league tables, examines why some independent schools no longer want anything to do with them', *Daily Telegraph*, 15 July 2002.

The effects of league tables: 'We can free ourselves from the tyranny of school league tables', Martin Stephen, *Daily Telegraph*, 29 April 2008.

Effect of SATs tests in the playground: 'A test that's failed; why put such stress on our kids?', Elizabeth Cook, *Daily Mirror*, 13 May 2008.

TESTING TIMES: HOW SCHOOLS HAVE BECOME MORE ABOUT
TESTING THAN LEARNING

How children develop maths anxiety: 'Education: Count to 10…and breathe deeply: Maths anxiety may affect 2 million children, and yet it is still poorly understood, leaving many struggling', Kate Brain, *Guardian*, 1 May 2012.

'Math performance and its relationship to math anxiety and metacognition', Angela M. Legg and Lawrence Locker Jr, *North American Journal of Psychology*, 1 November 2009. In another study – published in the journal *Behavioural and Brain Functions* – 433 British secondary school children aged 11 to 15 were presented with a maths test and asked to complete a questionnaire used to assess their physiological, emotional, cognitive and behavioural reactions to answering the questions. It found no difference between girls and boys in straight test results, but found that girls showed signs of more mathematical anxiety, July 2012. Scientists at the Stanford University School of Medicine have also found that brain function differs between people who have maths anxiety and those who don't. A series of MRI scans conducted on forty-six second- and third-grade students who did addition and subtraction revealed that those who feel panicky about doing maths had increased activity in regions associated with fear, which caused dampened activity in parts of the brain involved in problem-solving. Vinod Menon, the psychiatry professor who led the research says: 'The same part of the brain that responds to fearful situations, such as seeing a spider or snake, also shows a heightened response in children with high math anxiety.' The study was published in the journal *Psychological Science*, March 2012.

The flight-or-fight response in children's brains: Jenny Foster quotes, *ibid*.

HOW TIGER PARENTING AFFECTS OUR RELATIONSHIP WITH OUR CHILDREN

How children respond to parents if they feel loved conditionally on their success: The 2004 study on conditional love refers to research by Avi Assor, Guy Roth of Ben Gurion University and Edward L. Deci of the University of Rochester, who asked more than 100 college students whether the love they had received from their parents had seemed to depend on whether they did well at school, practised hard for sports, been considerate towards others or suppressed emotions like anger and fear. They found that children who got conditional approval were more likely to do what their parents wanted – but it came at a cost. These children were more likely to resent and dislike their parents. Their satisfaction when they did well also did not last long and they often felt ashamed and guilty. 'The Emotional Costs of Parents' Conditional Regard' was published the *Journal of Personality*. In a further piece of research, the researchers interviewed mothers of adult children. They found once again that conditional parenting was harmful because children who felt they were loved only when they lived up to their parents' expectations felt less worthy as adults.

Creation of false self: The University of Denver study, by S. Harter, D.B. Marold, N.R. Whitesell and G. Cobbs, called 'A model of the effects of perceived parent and peer support on adolescent false self behavior', was published in *Child Development*, April 1996.

Children feel more negative emotions towards controlling mothers: Affectionate, less controlling mothers have strongest relationships with their children, based on the paper 'Patterns of Maternal Directiveness by Ethnicity among Early Head Start Research Participants', published in *Parenting: Science and Practice* by researchers at the University of Missouri's MU College of Human Environmental Sciences, 4 February 2013.

Oliver James's views on conditional love: See reading list.

HOW COMPETITION AFFECTS RELATIONSHIPS BETWEEN CHILDREN

Effect of competitive reality TV: A study by researchers at Brigham Young University, US, published in the June 2010 issue of the *Journal of Broadcasting and Electronic Media*, found reality TV contains, on average, eighty-five verbal attacks, insults and snide remarks each hour – almost twice that seen in comedies, dramas or soaps. The study also found half the incidents were encouraged by producers baiting participants into bitching against their rivals.

HOW COMPETITIVENESS RUINS OUR EXPERIENCE OF PARENTING

Pressured parents syndrome: Described in *Pressured Parents, Stressed-Out Kids: Dealing with Competition While Raising a Successful Child*, Wendy S. Grolnick and Kathy Seal, Prometheus Books, 2008.

HOW SCHOOLS TURN UP THE TEMPERATURE

Difficulties of parents finding places at their preferred schools: 'The state school scramble: 13 applicants per place as thousands set to miss out on preferred choice', Sarah Harris, *Daily Mail*, 1 March 2013.

Parents move house to get the school they want: Around one in three – thirty-two per cent – of professional parents with children aged five to sixteen have moved to an area which they thought had good schools, and eighteen per cent have moved to live in the catchment area of a specific school, according to a new Sutton Trust report, 'Parent Power?'; research by Professor Becky Francis, of King's College London, and Professor Merryn Hutchings, of London Metropolitan University, drew on YouGov interviews with 1,173 parents of school-age children, 18 December 2013.

'Police called as parents cause havoc at grammar school exam', Tim Ross, *Evening Standard*, 10 October 2008.

Parents suffering heart palpitations: Janette Wallis of The Good Schools Guide, quoted in '£100-an-hour tutors, children being woken up at 5am to study. Meet the parents who will do anything to get their offspring into grammar school', Julia Llewellyn Smith, *Daily Mail*, 12 October 2011. Tutor Stephanie Williams' quote about stress on children. *Ibid.*

Parents turn to spying: 'Revealed: the legal loophole letting pushy parents "rent" the best state school places', Joshi Herrmann, *Evening Standard*, 14 October 2013.

Mother faked identity in bid to cheat girl of school place: Mark Blunder, *Evening Standard*, July 9, 2010.

THE SPORTING TIGER PARENT

Between the ages of twelve and sixteen, between eighty and ninety per cent of children drop out of organised sports, especially highly competitive sports: See *Sports, Youth and Character. A Critical Survey*, Robert K. Fullinwider, Institute for Philosophy and Public Policy, University of Maryland, 2006.

Dr Clifton Evers, a research fellow at the University of New South Wales, Australia, also says pushy parents are one of the main reasons children drop out of sport. Evers says the ninety children aged ten to sixteen who were interviewed for the study 'overwhelmingly resent parents who scream at them or make them do things they don't want to do – and they critique their parents with other kids because of it. Some kids spoke about "hating" their dads for being overbearing. That's very strong language to use.' Paul Connolly, *Sun Herald*, 15 June 2008.

HOW TIGER PARENTING AFFECTS OUR RELATIONSHIPS

Stressed parents create stressed kids: *Kids Pick Up On Everything – How parental stress is toxic to kids*, David Code, Createspace, September 2011.

PART THREE – How to shed your tiger parenting stripes

The birth of baby milestones: 'Why I fear for modern mothers', Heidi Murkoff (author of the world's best-selling baby book), *Daily Mail*, 13 March 2013.

UK children reading too early: Pushing reception pupils too hard could put them off reading for life, especially boys, according to Professor Lilian Katz, Professor of Education at the University of Illinois in the US, speaking at an international conference on foundation-stage learning at the University of Oxford, November 2007.

Better get used to it: The concept of 'better get used to it', described in 'Getting Hit on the Head: Lessons Justifying Bad Educational Practices as Preparation for More of the Same', Alfie Kohn, *Education Week*, 7 September 2005. Also see 'Working mother figures', the Office for National Statistics 'Women in the Labour Market' report, 25 September 2013. Working parents feel they neglect children: Almost half worry they are not good enough parents and have just half an hour of time for their children a night, according to a study of 2000 parents by OnePoll for Ribena, April 2013.

How much children own: Discussed in 'What really makes our children happy? They clamour for the latest video games and clothes but, says Dr Tessa Livingstone, they secretly yearn for much simpler pleasures', *Sunday Telegraph*, 18 September 2011.

'Babies inherit mums' stress', Sharon Labi, *The Sunday Times* (Australia), 1 March 2009, based on studies of 100 women during pregnancy and for six months after they gave birth at Sydney's Royal Hospital for Women.

Parents regret not spending more time with their kids: 'Two thirds of parents admit they would do things differently if they could have the time again', *Daily Mail*, 14 September 2012, based on research commissioned by Huggies.

UK employees work some of the longest hours in Europe: According to figures in an official report released by the Office for National Statistics in December 2011, full-timers in the UK worked 42.7 hours per week compared with the EU average of 41.6 hours.

Stressed parents risk having burnt-out children: 'Parents who suffer work stress risk passing on their worries to their children, causing them to burn out as well', *Daily Telegraph*, 21 January 2010. Researchers from the University of Jyväskylä, Finland, questioned more than 500 teenagers about whether they had ever experienced burn-out. Symptoms include tiredness, a sense of not being good enough and cynicism about the value of schooling. Their parents were asked similar questions about work-related stress. Researchers found that career disillusionment felt by mothers and fathers can be 'contagious', leading their offspring to lose interest in schoolwork. Published in the *European Journal of Developmental Psychology*, 2010.

Stress is passed to children: David Code, *ibid*.

How to identify when you are burnt-out: *Fried: Why You Burn Out and How to Revive*, Joan Borysenko, Hay House, 2011.

MAKING YOUR HOME INTO A REFUGE

Effects of stress and lack of sleep on exam results: 'Don't overlook childhood depression', Lauren Louters, *Journal of the American Academy of Physician's Assistants*, 1 September 2004. Also see 'It's Smart to Sleep – classroom strategies from a neurologist', Dr Judy Willis, *Pyschology Today*, 6 May 2012.

Unstoppable rise of the TV dinner: 'Less than half the UK's families now regularly sit down at the table to eat', Katy Winter, *Daily Mail*, 5 November 2013. A study has revealed that only forty-nine per cent of families eat their evening meals at the dinner table every day, as TV dinners become increasingly commonplace. Researchers polled 713 parents to discover their mealtime habits, and found that more than one in ten – fourteen per cent – of families revealed that they never eat meals together because family mealtimes face 'a three-pronged attack from television, technology and relentless work schedules'.

The positive effects of families eating together: Just the act of joining family members at the table makes the youngsters feel valued and has a positive effect on their emotional well-being, according to a study of 26,000 children aged between 11 and 15 by psychiatrists at Canada's McGill University, published in the *Journal of Adolescent Health*, March 2013. A Reader's Digest poll of 2,130 high school seniors shows that strong families give students a huge edge in academic performance. The poll found that students who regularly shared meals with their families scored higher on a special academic test than those who didn't. Of those who said their 'whole family sits around a table together for a meal' at least four times a week, sixty per cent got high scores and their results fell with the number the times children ate together.

Rising numbers of people say they are middle class: 'Seven out of ten people now view themselves as belonging to Middle Britain, compared with a quarter a generation ago', *ibid*.

Not enough exercise causes depression in children: 'Overload of screen time "causes depression in children"; study claims there is a link between too much television and computer game-playing and lower self-esteem in the young', Ian Burrell, *Independent*, 28 August 2013, based on a report by Public Health England which found that 'in the UK, 62 per cent of 11-year-olds, 71 per cent of 13-year-olds and 68 per cent of 15-year-olds report watching more than two hours of TV a day on weekdays, compared to Switzerland where the figure is less than 35 per cent across all three age groups'.

Exercise relieves depression in teens: According to researchers at the University of Newcastle, teens who had trainer-led workouts three times a week for twelve weeks had significant boosts in mood, and the severity of their depression was cut by sixty-three per cent. Eighty-three per cent of the teens who completed the exercise programme were no longer as depressed by the end of the study, which was presented at the Society for Neuroscience annual meeting in San Diego, November 2013.

Exercise improves memory: Physical exercise can improve primary school pupils' memories and help them to learn. The effect of fitness on mental recall was particularly potent when the information being learnt was challenging, according to the study by the University of Illinois, published in the scientific journal *PLOS ONE*, September 2013. Dr Lauren Raine asked forty-eight children aged between nine and ten to remember the names and locations on a made-up map either by studying the information or being tested on the material as they absorbed it. Half the children were in the top thirty per cent of their age group on a test measuring aerobic fitness, while the other half scored in the lowest thirty per cent. When asked to remember the information studied, children who were fitter performed better than those who were not as fit.

Pets calm children: In one study by Friedmann, Katcher, Thomas, Lynch and Messent (1983) cited in *Pets and the Family* by Marvin B. Sussman, thirty-six children aged between nine and sixteen were asked to read aloud from a book – once in the presence of a dog and once without. Their blood pressure and pulse rate were significantly lower when the dog was present.

Mind your language

A ratio of five positive interactions to every negative one is the best way to help your child feel confident and flourish. See *Before Happiness: Five Actionable Strategies to Create a Positive Path to Success*, Shawn Achor, Virgin, 2013.

HOW TO TACKLE NEGATIVE SELF-TALK

Mind Maps for Kids: Study Skills, Tony Buzan, Harper Thorsons, 2008.

GIVING THE RIGHT SORT OF PRAISE

Carol Dweck, *ibid.*

Children should compete with themselves: Noël Janis-Norton, interview with the author.

WHY WE HAVE TO STAY CONNECTED

Reconnecting with your child through Love Bombing: Psychologist Oliver James recommends a technique called Love Bombing. See his book on the subject: *Love Bombing: Reset Your Child's Emotional Thermostat*, Karnac Books, 2012.

How childhood optimism can protect against adult depression: See Martin Seligman's book *The Optimistic Child: A Proven Program to Safeguard Children Against Depression and Build Lifelong Resilience*, Houghton Mifflin, 1995.

Why emotional intelligence is important: For more on Daniel Goleman, see *Building Emotional Intelligence: Techniques to cultivate inner strength in children*, by Linda Lantieri and Daniel Goleman, Soundstrue, 2008 and *Emotional Intelligence: Why it Can Matter More Than IQ*, Daniel Goleman, Bloomsbury, 1996.

The Pale Blue Dot: For Carl Sagan's Pale Blue Dot clip, go to https://www.youtube.com/watch?v=p86BPM1GV8M.

Hugging for twenty seconds increasing oxytocin levels: 'Effects of partner support on resting oxytocin, cortisol, norepinephrine, and blood pressure before and after warm partner contact', K.M. Grewen, S.S. Girdler, J. Amico, K.C. Light, *Psychosomatic Medicine*, July 2005.

THE HOMEWORK BATTLE

Homework load has got heavier: Sue Hallam view's on homework from 'New term, new battle over homework', Katherine Sellgren, BBC News, 24 September 2013.

Heavy school bags partly to blame for rise in childhood back problems: 'Early injury often leads to adult pain', Julia McWatt, *Western Mail*, 3 September 2012. According to the British Chiropractic Association, seventy-two per cent of children said they carried around heavy books and sports equipment on their backs, but only a third said they wore their rucksack on both shoulders to distribute the weight evenly, October 2008.

More than one in four parents plan to hire tutors during the summer holiday: According to a survey of 1,000 parents by Mathsfactor.com.

Keeping the boundaries around homework in order to keep it conflict free: For more tips, see *Calmer, Easier, Happier Homework: The Revolutionary Programme That Transforms Homework*, Noël Janis-Norton, Hodder & Stoughton, 2013.

'Homework's Diminishing Returns', Harris Cooper, *New York Times*, 10 December 2010. (Cooper is author of *The Battle Over Homework*, Corwin, 2007.) See also *The Homework Myth, Why Our Children Get Too Much*, Alfie Kohn, Da Capo, 2007.

EXTRA-CURRICULAR ACTIVITIES

Children are overscheduled: 'The tyranny of the Tiger Mother: Exhausted children are "working" for more than 54 hours a week', *Daily Mail*, 5 September 2013, based on a survey of 2,000 parents by Haliborange.

When overscheduling becomes problematic: Dr Suniya Luthar says that she has no problem with extra-curricular activites but worries when parents over-scrutinise their children's performance in these activities. 'You don't just play soccer for fun or play stickball in the cul-de-sac, you're vying for the travel team by second grade. The only place where I say stop is where the child starts to say his or her performance determines his or her self-worth: I am as I can perform.' From 'Overscheduled Children – How Big A Problem?', *New York Times*, 11 October 2013.

Alarms raised over overscheduling: *Children of Fast-track Parents*, Andrée Aelion Brooks, Viking Books, 1989.

Children's cognitive performance increases when they spend less time in regimented whole-group activities and more time in free play: See *The Benefits of Recess in Primary School*, Anthony D. Pellegrini and Catherine M. Bohn-Gettler, Scholarpedia, 2013.

A WORD ON TEENS

When to talk to teens about university: *The Blessing of a B Minus: Using Jewish Teachings to Raise Resilient Teenagers*, Wendy Mogel, Scribner, 2011.

FINDING YOUR CHILD'S SPARK

For more about finding your child's spark: *Sparks: How Parents Can Ignite the Hidden Strengths of Teenagers*, Dr Peter Benson, Jossey-Bass, 2008.

SHOW YOUR CHILD THE DIFFERENT WAYS OF BEING INTELLIGENT

'A high IQ is like height in a basketball player. It's how you use it that counts', David Perkins quotes: 'Having a high IQ doesn't necessarily mean you're smart. Far from it', Michael Bond, *New Scientist*, 31 October 2009.

Theories of Multiple Intelligence: See *Frames of Mind: The Theory of Multiple Intelligences*, Howard Gardner, Basic Books, 2011 and *Emotional Intelligence: Why it Can Matter More Than IQ*, Daniel Goleman, Mass Market, 1996.

THE IMPORTANCE OF PLAY

The area around their homes where children are allowed to roam has dropped by ninety per cent since the 1970s: From 'Save children's relationship with the outdoors', National Trust, March 2013.

Just one in five UK children are 'connected to nature': Project by the Royal Society for the Protection of Birds (RSPB) involving academics from Essex based on questions to 1,000 UK eight- to twelve-year-olds.

Nature's lost generation: 'Fewer and fewer children today play outside and engage with the natural world. Studies show that this is having a huge impact on their health and development', Jon Henley, *Guardian*, 17 August 2010.

Conclusion

Harvard students become depressed when they achieve their dream: Positive psychologist and former college counsellor Shawn Achor on the disillusionment of Harvard students when they reach their goal: From 'Why you should be a Dolphin Parent (and not a Tiger Mum)', *The Times*, 21 September 2013. Achor says: 'About two weeks into their first term, their brains were no longer focused on the privilege of being at Harvard. Their brains were focused on the competition, the workload and the stress. Little setbacks overwhelmed them. Instead of being energised by the possibilities ahead, they shrank away from them.'

'Teacups' and 'crispies': From 'Hanging on to "baby"; many well-meaning parents who fear that Junior will miss out just can't back off, even as he grows up. The result: Everyone's stressed out', Mary MacVean, 11 March 2011.

'"Spoon-fed" students struggle to cope with demands of Oxbridge', *Daily Telegraph*, 11 December 2010, based on comments from Professor Guy Claxton, Co-Director of the Centre for Real-World Learning at Winchester University, who says Oxford and Cambridge were seeing a year-on-year rise in the number of young people who are 'lacking resilience, lacking the ability to cope if they do not get great success'.

One in every eight university students considers suicide: Based on a poll by the National Union of Students of 1,200 young people studying at universities across the UK. Overall, ninety-two per cent of respondents said they had suffered feelings of mental distress, including feeling down, stressed and demotivated. On average, respondents who reported feelings of mental distress experienced them once a month or more, and almost one-third suffered mental distress every week, May 2013.

Student suicide rates: Between 2007 and 2011, suicides by male students in full-time higher education grew by thirty-six per cent, from 57 to 78, while female student suicides almost doubled from 18 to 34, according to the Office of National Statistics , November 2013.

Young people feeling sense of worthlessness: The Prince's Trust charity said that twenty-one per cent of young people have experienced issues including suicidal thoughts, self-harm, panic attacks, insomnia and anger problems, January 2014.

'The question is not how intelligent are you, but how are you intelligent?': See Ken Robinson's video, www.youtube.com/watch?v=5oS9h3S3VK0.

FURTHER READING AND
SOURCES

Anderegg, David, *Worried All The Time: Overparenting in an Age of Anxiety and How to Stop it*, Free Press, 2003.

Chansky, Tama E., *Freeing Your Child From Negative Thinking*, Perseus Books, 2008.

Dweck, Carol, *Mindset: How You Can Fulfill Your Potential*, Robinson, February 2012.

Gray, Peter, *Free To Learn*, Basic Books, 2013.

Honoré, Carl, *Under Pressure: Putting the Child Back In Childhood*, Orion, 2009.

James, Oliver, *Britain On The Couch: How keeping up with the Joneses has depressed us since 1950*, Vermilion, 2010.

James, Oliver, *Love Bombing: Reset Your Child's Emotional Thermostat*, Karnac Books, 2012.

James, Oliver, *They F*** You Up: How to Survive Family Life*, Bloomsbury, 2006.

Janis-Norton, Noël, *Calmer, Easier, Happier Homework: The Revolutionary Programme That Transforms Homework*, Hodder & Stoughton, 2013.

Janis-Norton, Noël, *Calmer, Easier, Happier Parenting: The Revolutionary Programme That Transforms Family Life*, Hodder & Stoughton, 2012. For courses from Noël go to www.tnlc.info.

Levine, Madeline, *Teach Your Children Well: Why Values and Coping Skills Matter More Than Grades, Trophies, or 'Fat Envelopes'*, Harper Perennial, 2013.

Levine, Madeline, *The Price of Privilege: How Parental Pressure and Material Advantage Are Creating a Generation of Disconnected and Unhappy Kids*, Harper Paperbacks, 2008.

Mogel, Wendy, *The Blessing of a B Minus: Using Jewish Teachings to Raise Resilient Teenagers*, Scribner, 2011.

Palmer, Sue, *Toxic Childhood: How The Modern World Is Damaging Our Children And What We Can Do About It*, Orion, 2007.

Robinson, Ken, *Finding Your Element: How to Discover Your Talents and Passions and Transform Your Life*, Penguin, 2014.

Rosenfeld, Alvin and Wise, Nicole, *Hyperparenting: Are You Hurting Your Child by Trying Too Hard?*, St Martin's Press, 2000.

Schoenstein, Ralph, *My Kid's An Honor Student, Your Kid's A Loser: the Pushy Parent's Guide to Raising the Perfect Child*, Perseus Books, 2002.

Taylor, Charlie, *Divas and Dictators, The Secrets to Having a Much Better Behaved Child*, Vermilion, 2009.

ACKNOWLEDGEMENTS

With many thanks to all the following, as well as the many unnamed teachers, educators, parents, children and child psychologists who shared their experiences with me.

Thanks to:

Noël Janis-Norton, Jenny Foster, Caroline Montgomery, Carolyn Kerr, Mandy Goldsmith, Rachel Welch, Nadim and Carole Saad of www.bestofparenting.co.uk, Deanne Jade, Dr Nollaig Fenn, Professor Julian Elliott, Grendon Haines, Richard Gowthorpe, Christoph Harwood, Miriam Chachamu, Valerie Davis, Amanda Goodhart, Amanda Hayhurst, the Save Childhood Movement at www.savechildhood.net, Clive Hebard, Nikki Read, Giles Lewis, Barry Day, Christine Calland of www.notjustbehaviour.co.uk, and the lovely Simone Cave who told me to keep going with this book. You are missed.

INDEX